ISBN: 0-9826608-8-X
ISBN 13: 978-0-982-6608-8-1

You can visit us online at: **www.JacKrisPublishing.com**

Copyright 2011 by JacKris Publishing, LLC. All rights reserved. No part of this publication may be reproduced or transmitted in any form or by any means, electronic or mechanical, including photocopying, recording, or any information storage and/or retrieval system or device, without permission in writing from the publisher or as authorized by United States Copyright Law.

Printed in the United States of America.

Ver. 1.0.0-1

First Semester

Copyright 2011, Winning With Writing Level 7 – First Semester. All rights reserved.

Preface

We have designed this thorough program to be user friendly for both teacher and student. This program is arranged in **36 weekly lessons**. Lessons 1 through 18 are contained in this First Semester book. Lessons 19-36 are contained in *Winning With Writing*, Level 7, Second Semester book. Each lesson consists of five exercises labeled **Day 1** through **Day 5**.

Writing is very similar to other things in life; you need to have a plan and be well organized before you start. For example, you would never think of building a house without first having blueprints (plans) that clearly define the layout of the house. Without first having a plan, the house would certainly end up as a disconnected, unorganized mess.

In other words, you need to be organized before doing anything that is not obvious or simple. As I mentioned, being prepared before starting the actual drafting process is necessary. When writing we organize our writing by adhering to the following processes:

Outlining Process
1. The student first thinks of an idea (main topic) about which he wants to write.
2. The student then thinks of details that support his main topic. Instead of placing these details on a blank piece of paper, we provide a rough outline form when needed. This rough outline form is simply a place where general ideas are written in an organized manner. Completing the rough outline is the first step in organizing your writing.
3. After the student is through placing his ideas on the rough outline, it is used to build a final outline. It is during the transfer of information from the rough outline to the final outline that the details contained on the rough outline are further organized and developed into sentences for the actual writing assignment.

Drafting Process
1. The final outline is used as a guide to write a rough draft of the writing assignment. Typically, the student merely transfers the information contained on the final outline to the rough draft of the writing.
2. The student then edits the rough draft for grammar and content.
3. The final draft of the writing assignment is then written.

We believe this process is the easiest and most straight-forward way to write any type of writing. By using these processes, the difficult task of writing becomes extremely simple and easy for anyone. The processes taught in this book can be used for any type of writing of any length ranging from a single paragraph to an entire book.

Copyright 2011, Winning With Writing Level 7 – First Semester. All rights reserved.

Level 7 - First Semester

Table of Contents

Lesson 1 - Main Topic, Details, and Staying on Topic 1

Lesson 2 - The Writing Process 7

Lesson 3 - Sequence of Events and Time Order Words 19

Lesson 4 - Personal Narrative 27

Lesson 5 - Personal Narrative 40

   Lesson 6 - Review of Lessons 1-5 53

Lesson 7 - Spatial Organization, Comparing Objects, and Comparing Characters 60

Lesson 8 - Simile, Metaphor, Analogy, Personification, and Allusion 68

Lesson 9 - Alliteration, Onomatopoeia, Hyperbole, and Oxymoron 74

Lesson 10 - Descriptive Writing 82

Lesson 11 - Descriptive Writing 96

   Lesson 12 - Review of Lessons 7-11 109

Lesson 13 - Parts of a Creative Story 115

Lesson 14 - Quotations, Dialogue, Point of View, and Voice 129

Lesson 15 - Creative Writing 138

Lesson 16 - Creative Writing 159

Lesson 17 - Creative Writing 180

   Lesson 18 - Review of Lessons 13-17 201

Copyright 2011, Winning With Writing Level 7 – First Semester. All rights reserved.

Student's Name: _____

Winning With Writing Level 7

First Semester

Copyright 2011, Winning With Writing Level 7 – First Semester. All rights reserved.

Date:_____

Main Topic, Details, and Staying on Topic

A **main topic** is a thought or idea that provides general guidance for a writing. A main topic tells what the writing will be about. A main topic is not necessarily a complete sentence; it can be any thought ranging from a sentence or more, to a single word.

A. Write an **X** on the lines below which are acceptable as main topics.

1. _X_ submarines
2. _X_ cats
3. ___ the process of blacktopping a driveway
4. _X_ how to fix a car
5. _X_ clouds

B. What is the **main topic** of the four sentences below?

1. There are many types of nails that are used to build houses.
2. Lumber used to build a deck must be pressure treated.
3. Shingles need to be of high quality if the roof is going to last.
4. Make sure to use thick insulation to ensure efficient heating and cooling.

What is needed to build houses.

C. If we were to add the following sentence to the four sentences above, would it fit appropriately into a paragraph? Circle the correct answer.

Cinder blocks and mortar are used to build a strong foundation.

(yes) or no

Level 7, Lesson 1 – Main Topic, Details, and Staying on Topic

Date:_____

Main Topic, Details, and Staying on Topic

A. Which of the following sentences would **not** belong in a paragraph with the given **main topic**? Write an **X** by each sentence that does not belong.

1. Main Topic: **educational subjects**

    a.____ I am taking algebra this year.

    b._X_ My neighbor is Ms. Walters.

    c._X_ A good writing course will help me communicate more effectively.

    d.____ History is one of my favorite subjects.

2. Main Topic: **countries**

    a.____ Venezuela is located in South America.

    b.____ Canada is located in North America.

    c._X_ Asia is a large continent.

    d.____ Japan is a small country located in Asia.

3. Main Topic: **types of food**

    a.____ Italian foods usually include a lot of pasta based dishes.

    b.____ Japanese foods usually have fresh fish and vegetables as ingredients.

    c.____ American cuisine is varied and uses a lot of beef and vegetables.

    d._X_ Some fields are used to grow plants that yield high levels of sugar for bio-fuels.

4. Main Topic: **modes of transportation**

    a._X_ I mow the lawn every week with my father.

    b.____ Spaceships travel through space.

    c.____ My two feet will take me anywhere I wish to go.

    d.____ A unicycle is tricky but fun to ride.

Level 7, Lesson 1 – Main Topic, Details, and Staying on Topic

Date: _____

Main Topic, Details, and Staying on Topic

All writings have a main topic and details that make up the writing. Even the smallest single paragraph has a main topic (unless it is a rambling nonsensical paragraph). Of course all writings have details that form the body of the writing.

Regardless of the type of writing, it will consist of one or more paragraphs. Each paragraph should have the following three parts: a **topic sentence**, **detail sentences**, and an **ending sentence**.

The first sentence of a paragraph is usually the **topic sentence**. It is slightly indented (to the right) in relation to the rest of the paragraph. The **topic sentence** tells **generally** what the paragraph is about, but it does not provide specific detail about the paragraph. The topic sentence's primary purpose is to get the attention of the reader.

The **detail sentences** come after the topic sentence and form the **body** of the paragraph. The **body** of the paragraph is perhaps the most important part of the paragraph since it contains the detail of what the paragraph is about. All detail sentences should be related to the **topic sentence**, which means that the **detail sentences** should only discuss things that are suggested by the **topic sentence**. Making sure that the **detail sentences** and **topic sentence** are related within a paragraph is called **staying on topic**.

The **ending sentence** restates the topic sentence (using different words) and can also summarize the information contained in the detail sentences.

A. Answer the following questions.
1. Which part of a paragraph is probably the most important?
    a. detail sentences
    b. topic sentence
    c. ending sentence
    ⓓ the main topic

Level 7, Lesson 1 – Main Topic, Details, and Staying on Topic

2. What is a topic sentence supposed to do?
   a. It tells the reader all about the following paragraph. *(circled)*
   b. It summarizes the paragraph before it.
   c. It provides an ending to the ending sentence.
   d. It grabs the attention of the reader.

3. What is the goal of the detail sentences?
   a. to physically fit into the paragraph
   b. to stay on topic with the topic sentence *(circled)*
   c. to set up the ending sentence
   d. to have at least ten words

4. What is the body of a paragraph made from?
   a. detail sentences *(circled)*
   b. topic sentences
   c. the topic sentence and the detail sentences
   d. none of the above

B. Circle the following main topic that would be the best fit for each paragraph below.
   1. I like to sit on the swing on the back porch and watch the world go by. Right behind my house is a busy road. I can watch the many different types of cars, trucks, bicycles, and people moving by. Sometimes my whole family sits on the porch and watches the clouds roll in. Sometimes this means a storm is on the way. As soon as it starts raining, we go inside.
      a. things to do outside
      b. things my family likes to do together
      c. we like watching things as we sit on the swing *(circled)*
      d. swings are a great place to sit

   2. Picking a place to eat can be a big job. First of all you have to ask those who will be dining with you if they have a preference for a particular type of food. Next, you need to decide how much time you have to eat your meal (fast food or a sit-down dinner). Then, you need to decide how much money you want to spend on dinner. Lastly, you need to find out if there are any restaurants nearby that satisfy the answers to the preceding questions.
      a. going out to eat is fun
      b. it can be hard to find the right restaurant *(circled)*
      c. some people do not like eating the same things as others
      d. it's easy to find a place to eat where everyone agrees

Date: _____

Main Topic, Details, and Staying on Topic

A. Write your own topic sentence and an ending sentence for the main topic **pizza**.

Topic Sentence:

How to make pizza.

Write your own four detail sentences for the main topic **pizza**.

1. First make pizza crust. Then shape it into a circle and put on a circle pizza pan.

2. Now you spred the sauce, put cheese on and the topings of your choosing.

3. Next your gonna put the pizza in the oven and let it cook.

4. Then you take your pizza outta the oven and let it cool down.

B. Ending Sentence:

Now you have made homemade pizza.

Main Topic, Details, and Staying on Topic

Date: _____

A. Use the information you wrote during Day 4 about pizza to write a paragraph. Start the paragraph by writing the topic sentence, followed by the detail sentences, and then finally the ending sentence.

How to make pizza.
First make pizza crust. Then shape it into a circle and put on a circle pizza pan. Now you spread the sauce, put cheese on and the toppings of your choosing. Next your gonna put the pizza in the oven and let it cook. Then you take the pizza outta the oven and let it cool down. Now you have made homemade pizza.

Date: _____

The Writing Process

In the last lesson you simply wrote a paragraph by making up a topic sentence, some detail sentences, and an ending sentence. Writing a decent paragraph is not too hard when you are only writing a single paragraph. On the other hand, when tasked with writing multiple paragraphs (such as a story) it becomes much easier when you first organize your thoughts before writing. Organizing your thoughts in writing before actually starting your writing assignment is called **outlining**.

Even though it is probably unnecessary to arrange your thoughts before writing a single paragraph, for simplicity purposes we will discuss the outlining process, and then the writing process, for a single paragraph.

To create a paragraph (or more than one paragraph), there are two processes that should be performed in order, the **outlining process** and then the **drafting process**.

Outlining is the **act of gathering information** necessary to complete the **rough outline** and a **final outline**. For your use, the rough outline form is located at the end of today's lesson. The final outline form is located at the end of the next day's lesson.

The drafting process is where the information gathered during the outlining process is used to write the actual paragraph.

Below is the writing process for writings other than creative stories.

- <u>Outlining Process</u>
  A. Complete the rough outline
  B. Complete the final outline

- <u>Drafting Process</u>
  A. Complete the rough draft
  B. Edit the rough draft
  C. Complete the final draft

Level 7, Lesson 2 – The Writing Process

Outlining Process

Complete the rough outline

The outlining process starts by filling out the rough outline. After the rough outline is complete, the information it contains will be used to develop a final outline. The final outline will then be used as a guide to complete the writing. Below is a sample rough outline that shows its parts:

Rough Outline

- Main Topic
- Details (used to make detail sentences)
    - Detail #1:
    - Detail #2:
    - Detail #3:

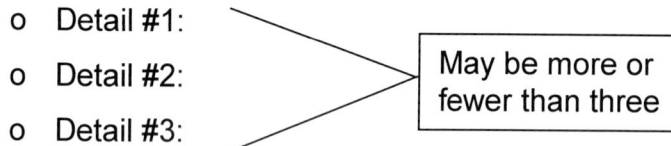
May be more or fewer than three

Step #1 (develop the main topic)

The first piece of information needed to complete the rough outline is a **main topic**. A main topic is a **very general idea** that tells what a paragraph is about. Let's assume we have decided that we want to write a paragraph about **jungle animals**. This bolded phrase is called the **main topic** of the paragraph. Notice that we called this a phrase and not a sentence? As we learned in Lesson 1, a main topic does not have to be a sentence.

A. You will now decide on a different main topic for the paragraph you will write. You can write about **your favorite animal, your favorite sport,** or **your favorite school subject**. Write your main topic in the **main topic** section of your rough outline found at the end of this day's lesson.

Step #2 (develop details)

Now that you have a main topic written on the rough outline, you need to think of **details** to complete the rough outline. A detail can be a thought, phrase, or sentence that provides information about the main topic. These details will later be turned into **detail sentences** for the **final outline**.

Assume we possess no knowledge of our example jungle animals, so we conducted some research to gather information. You can use resources you already have, the library, the Internet, or other dependable sources.

Our research returned the following **details** about jungle animals:

1. parrots
2. frogs
3. monkeys

These are **details** because they provide more description to the main topic of **jungle animals**. For our example, our rough outline would look like this:

Rough Outline
- Main Topic:
  o jungle animals
- Details (used to make detail sentences)
  o parrots
  o frogs
  o monkeys

B. Think of a few details for your main topic (from the choices you were given on the previous page) and write them on the **details** section of the rough outline. With the addition of your **details**, your rough outline is complete.

Rough Outline

Main Topic:
Horses

Details: (used to make detail sentences)
- short
- Tall
- big
- small
- fury

The Writing Process

Complete the final outline

We will now start organizing our paragraph by completing a final outline with the following structure:

Final Outline

- Topic Sentence:

- Detail Sentences: (constructed from details in the rough outline)
    - Detail Sentence #1:
    - Detail Sentence #2: *May be more or fewer than three*
    - Detail Sentence #3:

- Ending Sentence: (restates the topic sentence and/or summarizes the detail sentences.)

Step #1 (develop a topic sentence)

The first step to completing a final outline is developing a **topic sentence**. A topic sentence tells **generally** what the paragraph is about, but it does not provide specific detail about the paragraph. Its primary purpose is to get the attention of the reader.

We can use the **main topic** and the **details** written on the rough outline to write a **topic sentence** for the final outline. While the **main topic** on the rough outline may not be a complete sentence, the **topic sentence** in the final outline must be a complete sentence. Using our example main topic of **jungle animals**, our topic sentence could be something like the following: **There are many different types of colorful and dangerous animals living in the jungle**. Write your topic sentence in the space provided on the final outline found at the end of this day's lesson.

Step #2 (develop detail sentences)

The next piece of information needed to build the final outline is detail sentences. Detail sentences will make up the greatest portion of your writing. They actually tell the story of the paragraph. This makes the detail sentences the most important part of the writing.

Look at the **details** written on the rough outline, it is our goal to use these **details** along with the **main topic** and **topic sentence** to think of interesting detail sentences for the paragraph. While you are thinking of **detail sentences**, remember that they will all need to fit together as a paragraph. By the time you are done you should have several detail sentences written under the **detail sentences** section of the final outline. Make sure to place the detail sentences in the correct order if there is a required order for your writing.

Since you now have all of the information you need to think of detail sentences, write your detail sentences in the detail sentences section of the final outline.

After looking at our details, main topic, and topic sentence from our example (jungle animals), we added some detail sentences to our final outline. Our final outline now looks like this:

Final Outline

Topic Sentence:
   There are many different types of colorful and dangerous animals living in the jungle.
Detail Sentences:
   -Scarlet macaws are known for their beauty. These parrots have stunning colors and long tails. When raised in captivity, these birds can be trained to speak by mimicking sounds they hear over and over.
   -Dart frogs are a group of small colorful frogs that live in jungles. Unlike most frogs, which are more active at night, these frogs are brightly colored and tend to move about mostly during the day. Some types of these frogs are now endangered because they have been excessively hunted for their poisonous secretions, which are rubbed onto darts for hunting.
   -There are many different types of monkeys that live in the jungle. By having hands with opposable thumbs, they are terrific climbers, so they are right at home in the jungle. Nuts and berries are also abundant in the jungle, which are major sources for their food.
Ending Sentence: (not developed yet)

Step #3 (developing an ending sentence)

The last step to complete the final outline is to create an **ending sentence**. It is the function of the ending sentence to restate the topic sentence or summarize the detail sentences. For our example we could write the following ending sentence:

As you can see, there are many types of animals that make their home in the jungle.

Create an ending sentence for your paragraph and write it in the **ending sentence** section of your final outline. With the addition of the ending sentence, the final outline is complete.

Final Outline

Topic Sentence:

Stuff about horses.

Detail Sentences:

Horses can be very tall or very short. Horses are large or small animals. They have lots of fur. They also can have long or short manes.

Ending Sentence: (written after the topic sentence and detail sentences)

Horses are cool animals.

Date: _____

The Writing Process

Drafting Process

<u>Complete the rough draft</u>

So far you have spent quite a bit of time completing the rough outline and the final outline. As a result, your final outline has all of the necessary pieces to complete your writing.

If you think of something you want to add while you are writing your rough draft, now is a great time to do so. The final outline will now be used as a guide to write a rough draft.

Start by writing your **topic sentence** first on the lines below. Next, write the **detail sentences** in the order which they occur in your final outline. Finish your paragraph with the **ending sentence**.

Observations of horses. Horses can be very tall or very short. Horses can be large or small animals. They have lots of fun. They also can have long or short manes. Horses are cool animals.

Date: _____

The Writing Process

Edit the rough draft

It is now time to **edit** the rough draft you wrote on Day 3. Use the editing marks shown in **Appendix C** to correct any mistakes.

Do your paragraphs say what you want them to say? Do the words you chose make sense?

Look for and fix the following errors: 1) incorrectly used, misspelled, or misplaced words, 2) incorrect or missing spacing, 3) incorrect, missing, or misplaced punctuation, and 4) incorrect or missing capitalization.

The Writing Process

Date: _____

Complete the final draft

On Day 4 you edited your paragraph. Today you will rewrite your paragraph in its final draft form.

Read your paragraphs one more time. Do your sentences flow well from one to the other? Does your paragraph make sense? Can you make it even better by adding 1) **strong verbs**, 2) **adverbs**, 3) **exact nouns**, or 4) **descriptive adjectives**? Rewrite your edited paragraph below.

Observations of horses. Horses can be very tall of very short. Horses can be large or small animals. They have lots of fur. They also can have long or short manes. There are many breeds of horses.

Sequence of Events and Time Order Words

Some events occur very randomly.

I went swimming. We went to visit my grandparents. I bought a new bicycle. My family went on many long walks together.

You can see how it doesn't really matter if these events are told in any particular order.

On the other hand, some things do need to be told in a certain order or sequence. If you were writing a story about building a house, this process would most likely need to be completed in a particular sequence. If you were writing a paragraph to explain this process, obviously your paragraph would not make sense if you wrote the steps in a random order. The word **sequence** means that things happen one at a time, one after the other.

A. Below are several steps, written randomly, that are necessary for planting vegetables in a garden. Obviously, some steps need to occur before others. Place the correct number (1-6) by each entry to show when it occurs in the process.

2 Remove any weeds or debris from the space where you would like to plant the seeds.

1 Buy seeds for the types of vegetables you want to grow.

5 Water the planted seeds.

3 Plow the cleared ground where the seeds will be planted.

4 Plant the seeds into the freshly plowed dirt, and cover the seeds with dirt.

6 When the vegetables are grown and ripe, harvest and enjoy them.

Level 7, Lesson 3 – Sequence of Events and Time Order Words

B. Now that you have identified the order for the previous process, write a paragraph with the steps in **part A** that explains how to plant vegetables in a garden. **Add your own step below to the steps already listed in part A.** Remember to add a topic sentence and an ending sentence. It is not necessary to perform outlining for this exercise.

Buy the seeds for the types of vegetable you want to grow. Remove any weeds or debris from the space where you would like to plant the seeds. Plow the cleared ground where the seeds will be planted. Plant the seeds in the freshly powed dirt, and cover the seeds with dirt. Water the planted seeds. When the vegetables are grown and ripe, harvest and enjoy them.

Sequence of Events and Time Order Words

Date: _____

In the exercise from Day 1 you wrote a paragraph about planting seeds in a garden. We have written below what the paragraph you wrote might look like.

> Raising food in a garden is very fun and satisfying. Buy seeds for the type of vegetables you want to grow. Remove any weeds and debris from the space where you would like to plant the seeds. Plow the cleared ground where the seeds will be planted. Plant the seeds into the freshly plowed dirt, and cover the seeds with dirt. Water the planted seeds. When the vegetables are grown and ripe, harvest and enjoy them. Vegetables from our garden are inexpensive compared to those bought in a supermarket, and my family thinks they taste much better.

The first thing you will notice is that the above paragraph is really made up of a few sentences that are simply added together. There really is no relation from one sentence to the next. For example, we don't know if certain steps can or should be performed at the same time, or if we need to wait a certain amount of time before performing a later step.

In order to connect sentences together and give them relation to each other, we use **time order** transitional words. Actually, time order words can make a paragraph **flow** better whether or not the story needs to be told in a specific order.

Any word that tells **when** can be a time order transitional word. The following table contains a sample of **time order** transitional words:

first	finally	yesterday	meanwhile	earlier
now	one day	Tuesday	two weeks ago	yearly
next	also	later	however	afterward
then	sometimes	soon	at last	eventually
soon thereafter	tomorrow	concurrently	once	at length
second	for a minute	initially	before	daily
at the same time	to begin with	subsequently	previously	immediately

Level 7, Lesson 3 – Sequence of Events and Time Order Words

Below are two paragraphs. One contains time order words and one does not.

Original Paragraph

Mom and Dad are throwing a birthday party for me. I will be thirteen years old and my parents want to celebrate me becoming a teenager. I helped Dad clean the house before our guests arrive. Mom made her famous three bean dip. Dad and I made pasta. I hope everyone has a nice time.

Modified Paragraph

Mom and Dad are throwing a birthday party for me **tomorrow**. I will be thirteen years old **in a few days** and my parents want to celebrate me becoming a teenager. **Yesterday** I helped Dad clean the house before our guests arrive. **Today**, Mom made her famous three bean dip **while** Dad and I made pasta. I hope everyone has a nice time.

Can you see how the second paragraph flows better than the first? By using time order words, the modified paragraph tells the reader when certain things happen within the paragraph. The paragraph is much easier to read with time order words, which is another way to say that it **flows** better. Also, you will notice that time order words do not necessarily have to be placed at the beginning of sentences.

A. Look at the paragraph you wrote on Day 1. Rewrite if below using **time order words**.

First buy the seeds for the types of vegetable you want to grow. Then remove any weeds or debris from the space where you would like to plant the seeds. Next plow the cleared ground where the seeds will be planted. Finally plant the seeds in the freshly plowed dirt and water the planted seeds. Now when the vegetables are grown and ripe, harvest and enjoy them.

Level 7, Lesson 3 – Sequence of Events and Time Order Words

Sequence of Events and Time Order Words

first	finally	yesterday	meanwhile	earlier
now	one day	Tuesday	two weeks ago	yearly
next	also	later	however	afterward
then	sometimes	soon	at last	eventually
soon thereafter	tomorrow	concurrently	once	at length
second	for a minute	initially	before	daily
at the same time	to begin with	subsequently	previously	immediately

A. Choose **time order** words from the box above to complete each sentence. Try to use each time order word only once.

1. _At the same time_ as Mom cleaned the counter, we swept the floor.

2. I ate a whole loaf of bread. _Later_ I felt sick.

3. _One day_ we got a new car for Mom.

4. After Glen knocked over the glass, he _immediately_ wiped it up.

5. Bob came in _first_, and Dan came in _second_ in the race.

6. _Yesterday_ he sold his house, but _tomorrow_ he will buy another.

7. The story teller spoke _at length_ about the historic battle.

8. _Initially_ Freeda was startled when the firecracker exploded.

9. _Soon_ we all got tired and fell asleep.

10. We all sang songs and cheered. _Finally_ we relaxed and went home.

11. _Two weeks ago_ there was a little girl who strolled through the forest wearing a red hood.

12. _Eventually_ it rained, but we went outside to play anyway.

13. _Once_ Ben hit the baseball. _Next_ he ran to first base.

14. The crowd looked at the pictures Erin took _subsequently_ during the event.

Level 7, Lesson 3 – Sequence of Events and Time Order Words

Date: _____

Sequence of Events and Time Order Words

A. Read the paragraph below and rewrite it to put it in correct **time order**.

⁷After that, we thoroughly mix the ingredients until it appears as a smooth ball of dough. ⁵Finally, we remove the bread from the oven. ¹First we combine flour, water, salt, sugar, yeast, and two eggs into a bowl. ³Next we cover the bowl with a paper towel to hold in the heat as the yeast starts to work by raising the dough. ⁴Afterwards, we set the oven to 375 degrees. ⁶After removing it from the oven, the bread is coated with a generous layer of butter.

First we combine flour, water, salt, sugar, yeast, and two eggs into a bowl. After that, we thoroughly mix the ingredients until it appears as a smooth ball of dough. Next we cover the bowl with a paper towel to hold in the heat as the yeast starts to work by raising the dough. Afterwards, we set the oven to 375 degrees. Finally, we remove the bread from the oven. After removing it from the oven, the bread is coated with a generous layer of butter.

Date: _____

Sequence of Events and Time Order Words

A. Write a paragraph with five sentences that tells about performing a task. Make sure that the task you select is one that needs to be performed in a specific order. Add your own **time order words** (such as first, next, then, and last) to show the order of your task. Also, make sure to write a topic sentence and an ending sentence for this exercise.

Protien balls.

First get peanut butter, honey, and protien ball mix. Next add all the ingridient's together. Now roll the dough into balls about a inch thick. Then put them on a plate. Finally put them in the fridge. Enjoy!

Date: _____

Personal Narrative

In this lesson you will write a six paragraph (one introductory paragraph, four subtopic paragraphs, and one concluding paragraph) personal narrative. A personal narrative is a **true story** about something that happened to you or something you did. A narrative can be about something very exciting or something very simple.

Audiences for a personal narrative can range from a friend, a parent, or even a teacher. The writer needs to keep his audience in mind as he chooses his words.

Why do people write personal narratives? Some people write them simply because they want to share an experience. Sometimes they write them to entertain the reader. Personal narratives can be happy, scary, sad, or any feeling in between.

Write a six paragraph personal narrative about **something in your life that happened that you initially thought was a bad thing, but it turned out to be a good thing**. Use the following steps to develop a personal narrative:

Outlining Process
 A. Complete the rough outline
 B. Complete the final outline

Drafting Process
 A. Complete the rough draft
 B. Edit the rough draft
 C. Complete the final draft

Outlining Process

We will now begin writing a personal narrative with the outlining process. Outlining is the process where information about the writing is gathered in order to complete the rough outline and a final outline.

The entire outlining process is explained in **Appendix B**. Since this is the first time you are developing a writing with more than one paragraph, you should turn to Appendix B and familiarize yourself with the outlining process for multiple paragraphs. The outlining process for multiple paragraphs really isn't that much different than the outlining process for single paragraphs. However, there are **some** differences that you need to know. Whether or not you use Appendix B, you still need to complete the rough outline and the final outline in this lesson.

Complete the rough outline

Rough Outline

Main Topic: Our roof collapsed.

Subtopic #1: Our roof collapsed
  Details: We thought that it would be bad at first.

Subtopic #2: Had to take the house down
  Details: Still bad.

Subtopic #3: rebuilt house
  Details: Starting to be good.

Subtopic #4: finishe house
  Details: It ended up being a blessing that the roof caved in.

Date: _____

Personal Narrative

Complete the final outline

Final Outline

Introductory Paragraph:

At first we thought having our roof collapse was a bad thing but we were wrong.

Subtopic #1:

Topic Sentence:

When it happened.

Detail Sentences:

The roof had caved into the living room. My parents had to decide whether they would rebuild or fix the roof. It turned out rebuilding the whole house would be more cost effective.

Level 7, Lesson 4 – Personal Narrative

Ending Sentence: (written after the topic sentence and detail sentences)

Things are getting better.

Subtopic #2:

Topic Sentence:

They found some things out about the house.

Detail Sentences:

As my parents were taking down the house they saw the wiring was bad and was rubbing against the insulation witch was a huge fire hazard.

Ending Sentence: (written after the topic sentence and detail sentences)

Things are looking good

Subtopic #3:

Topic Sentence:

The new house was built.

Detail Sentences:

My dad and a couple of buddies rebuilt the house frames and had everything up in 9 days.

Ending Sentence: (written after the topic sentence and detail sentences)

We now have an amazing new house.

Subtopic #4:

Topic Sentence:

Detail Sentences:

_____
_____
_____
_____
_____
_____
_____

Ending Sentence: (written after the topic sentence and detail sentences)

_____
_____
_____

Concluding Paragraph:

We live in our new house and are very thankful our roof caved in. It ended up being a big blessing.

Lesson 4 Day 3

Date: _____

Personal Narrative

Drafting Process

Complete the rough draft

So far you have spent quite a bit of time filling out the rough outline and the final outline. As a result, your final outline has all of the necessary pieces to complete your writing.

If you think of something you want to add while you are writing your rough draft, please do so. The final outline will now be used as a guide to write a rough draft.

Start by writing your **introductory paragraph**, sentences for each **subtopic** (topic sentence, detail sentences, and ending sentence), and **concluding paragraph** on the lines below.

At first we thought having our roof collapse was a bad thing but we were wrong. The roof had caved into the living room. My parents had to decide wether they would rebuild or fix the roof. It turned out rebuilding the whole house would be better. As my parents were taking down the house they saw the wiring was bad. My dad and a couple (2) of his buddies built the house (framework and walls) in 9 days. We live in our new house and are very thankful our roof collapsed. It ended up being a big blessing.

Level 7, Lesson 4 – Personal Narrative

Lesson 4 Day 4

Date: _____

Personal Narrative

<u>Edit the rough draft</u>

It is now time to **edit** the rough draft you wrote on Day 3. Use the editing marks shown in **Appendix C** to correct any mistakes.

Do your paragraphs say what you want them to say? Do the words you chose make sense?

Look for and fix the following errors: 1) incorrectly used, misspelled, or misplaced words, 2) incorrect or missing spacing, 3) incorrect, missing, or misplaced punctuation, and 4) incorrect or missing capitalization.

Lesson 4 Day 5

Date: _____

Personal Narrative

Complete the final draft

On Day 4 you edited your paragraph. Today you will rewrite your paragraphs in their final draft form.

Read your paragraphs one more time. Do your sentences flow well from one to the other? Does your entire story make sense? Can you make it even better by adding 1) **time order words**, 2) **strong verbs**, 3) **adverbs**, 4) **exact nouns**, or 5) **descriptive adjectives**? Rewrite your edited paragraphs below.

At first when our roof collapsed we thought it was a bad thing. Our roof caved into the living room. My parents had to decide whether to rebuild the house or fix the roof. It turned out rebuilding the house would be more cost effective. As my parents were taking the house down they saw the wiring was bad. My dad and 2 of his buddies rebuilt the house in 9 days. We live in our new house now. It ended up being a blessing our roof caved in.

Lesson 5 Day 1

Date: _____

Personal Narrative

Write another **personal narrative** that is **six** paragraphs in length. Write about **somewhere fun you go in the summer**. Describe this place and what you do there. Do you have any friends there? Think of a **main topic** for your personal narrative. Before you settle on a main topic, answer the following questions to yourself:

1. Is your idea something interesting that people will want to read?
2. Who is your audience? Depending on your audience, you may need to explain things in greater detail using simpler words.
3. Is your idea too broad? If your idea is too broad you will have too much material for the allotted size of your writing.
4. Is your idea too narrow? If your idea is too narrow you will not have enough material (content) for your writing.

We will now start the writing process for a **personal narrative**.

Outlining Process
    A. Complete the rough outline
    B. Complete the final outline

Drafting Process
    A. Complete the rough draft
    B. Edit the rough draft
    C. Complete the final draft

Outlining Process

We will now begin writing your personal narrative assignment with the outlining process. Outlining is the process where information about the writing is gathered in order to complete the rough outline and a final outline.

The entire outlining process is explained in **Appendix B**. If you need help in completing the rough outline or the final outline, use Appendix B. Whether or not you use Appendix B first, you still need to complete the rough outline found on the next page and the final outline found in the lesson on Day 2.

Complete the rough outline

Rough Outline

Main Topic:
In the summer we often go to our property on the hoko river.

Subtopic #1: Getting there
   Details: The drive is kind of long

Subtopic #2: Arriving
   Details: When we get out of the car we are in a field surrounded by trees

Subtopic #3: The river
   Details: The river is like a lazy river. Its very funny to play and snorkel in.

Subtopic #4: More of the river
   Details: This year we are gonna bring the horses out to swim them too.

Personal Narrative

Lesson 5 Day 2

Date: _____

Complete the final outline

Final Outline

Introductory Paragraph:

In the summer we often times go to our property on the hoho river in Sekiu.

Subtopic #1:

Topic Sentence:

The drive to Sekiu is kinda long.

Detail Sentences:

The drive is about 1hr and 15min long. We like to read books and listen to music and talk.

Ending Sentence: (written after the topic sentence and detail sentences)

The ride isn't too boring.

Subtopic #2:

Topic Sentence:

Once we get there we unpack.

Detail Sentences:

Unpacking and setting up is boring but afterwards it's lots of fun. We have to get our camp area set up and the horses area set up.

Ending Sentence: (written after the topic sentence and detail sentences)

It takes a lot of work to go camping.

Subtopic #3:

Topic Sentence:
Now we actually get to camp.

Detail Sentences:
We like to kayak and go fishing and ride horses and other stuff.

Ending Sentence: (written after the topic sentence and detail sentences)

Subtopic #4:

Topic Sentence:

Detail Sentences:

_____
_____
_____
_____
_____
_____
_____

Ending Sentence: (written after the topic sentence and detail sentences)

_____
_____
_____
_____

Concluding Paragraph:

_____
_____
_____
_____
_____

Lesson 5 Day 3

Date: _____

| Personal Narrative |

Drafting Process

Complete the rough draft

So far you have spent quite a bit of time filling out the rough outline and the final outline. As a result, your final outline has all of the necessary pieces to complete your writing.

If you think of something you want to add while you are writing your rough draft, please do so. The final outline will now be used as a guide to write a rough draft.

Start by writing your **introductory paragraph**, sentences for each **subtopic** (topic sentence, detail sentences, and ending sentence), and **concluding paragraph** on the lines below.

_____
_____
_____
_____
_____
_____
_____
_____
_____
_____
_____
_____
_____
_____
_____
_____
_____
_____

Lesson 5 Day 4

Personal Narrative

Date: _____

Edit the rough draft

It is now time to **edit** the rough draft you wrote on Day 3. Use the editing marks shown in **Appendix C** to correct any mistakes.

Do your paragraphs say what you want them to say? Do the words you chose make sense?

Look for and fix the following errors: 1) incorrectly used, misspelled, or misplaced words, 2) incorrect or missing spacing, 3) incorrect, missing, or misplaced punctuation, and 4) incorrect or missing capitalization.

Lesson 5 Day 5

Date: _____

Personal Narrative

Complete the final draft

On Day 4 you edited your paragraphs. Today you will rewrite your paragraphs in their final draft form.

Read your paragraphs one more time. Do your sentences flow well from one to the other? Does your entire story make sense? Can you make it even better by adding 1) **time order words**, 2) **strong verbs**, 3) **adverbs**, 4) **exact nouns**, or 5) **descriptive adjectives**? Rewrite your edited paragraphs below.

_____
_____
_____
_____
_____
_____
_____
_____
_____
_____
_____
_____
_____
_____
_____
_____
_____
_____
_____

Lesson 6 Review Day 1

Date: _____

Review of Main Topic, Details, and Staying on Topic

A. Answer each question below.

1. Read the following four sentences. What is the **main topic** of the four sentences?

    a. Bloodhounds are droopy eared dogs that are good at tracking scents.

    b. African elephants have huge droopy ears and excellent hearing.

    c. Lopped eared rabbits have long droopy ears that look cute.

    d. Brahman bulls have long droopy ears but are very mean.

    _____

2. Write a topic sentence for the four sentences above.

    _____
    _____
    _____

3. Assume that the four sentences above are detail sentences found in a final outline for a single paragraph. Write an appropriate ending sentence for the above sentences.

    _____
    _____
    _____

4. Would the following sentences fit into a paragraph with the sentences above? Circle the correct answers.

    a. yes or no   Believe it or not, even cornstalks can have droopy ears.

    b. yes or no   Some bats have very pointy ears but very good hearing.

    c. yes or no   The Boer goat from South Africa is also known for its droopy ears.

    d. yes or no   Horses do not have droopy ears, but they have excellent hearing.

Level 7, Lesson 6 - Review of Lessons 1-5

Lesson 6 Review Day 2

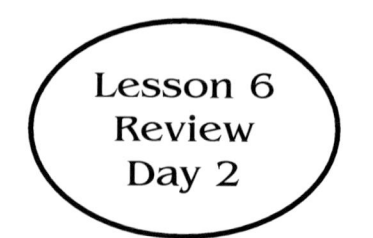

Date: _____

Review of the Writing Process

A. Answer the following questions.

1. When is a good time to add additional ideas or wording to your writing?

    a. when thinking of a topic sentence

    b. when transferring information from the rough outline to the final outline

    c. when completing the rough draft

    d. when writing the final draft

2. What is an ending sentence supposed to do?

    a. It restates the detail sentences by using different words.

    b. It describes the main topic.

    c. It summarizes the information in the detail sentences.

    d. It adds additional information.

3. What comes after a **main topic** is chosen?

    a. rough draft of the paragraph

    b. edit the rough draft

    c. outlining

    d. write an ending sentence

4. What is a single **paragraph** called in a multi paragraph final outline?

    a. rough draft of the paragraph

    b. edit the rough draft

    c. a subtopic

    d. write an ending sentence

Level 7, Lesson 6 - Review of Lessons 1-5

Lesson 6 Review Day 3

Review of Sequence of Events and Time Order Words

Date: _____

A. Place the correct number (1-7) by each entry to show when it occurs in the sequence of **changing a flat tire**.

___ Raise the vehicle into the air and remove the loosened lug nuts.

___ Slightly loosen the lug nuts of the flat tire with the vehicle still on the ground.

___ Remove the spare tire from the trunk and make sure it has appropriate air pressure.

___ Carefully lower the vehicle to the ground.

___ Position the spare on the vehicle and install the lug nuts snugly, but do not yet fully tighten them.

___ Fully tighten the lug nuts.

___ Remove the flat tire from the vehicle.

B. Read the paragraph below and rewrite it to put it in the correct **time order**.

    We thought about it for a minute, and then we said we wanted it as soon as possible. Within two days, our package came in the mail. After seeing the advertisement, Mom thought that we should get one. While placing our order, the operator asked how we wanted it shipped. Quickly, I rushed to get her credit card so we could order one right away. Last week I saw an interesting grill being sold on television during an infomercial.

_____
_____
_____
_____
_____
_____
_____
_____

Level 7, Lesson 6 - Review of Lessons 1-5

Lesson 6 Review Day 4

Date: _____

Review of Personal Narratives

In this exercise you will write a one paragraph personal narrative about **something you did around the house to help your mother or father**. Conduct some **outlining** by completing the rough outline below and final outline on the next page.

Rough Outline

Main Topic:

_____
_____
_____

Details: (used to make detail sentences)

_____
_____
_____
_____
_____
_____
_____
_____
_____
_____
_____
_____
_____

Level 7, Lesson 6 - Review of Lessons 1-5

Final Outline

Topic Sentence:

_____
_____
_____
_____

Detail Sentences:

_____
_____
_____
_____
_____
_____
_____
_____

Ending Sentence: (written after the topic sentence and detail sentences)

_____
_____
_____

Lesson 6 Review Day 5

Review of Personal Narratives

Date: _____

A. Use the final outline you made on Day 4 of this lesson to complete a rough draft of your personal narrative.

_____
_____
_____
_____
_____
_____
_____
_____
_____
_____
_____
_____
_____
_____
_____
_____
_____
_____
_____
_____
_____
_____
_____
_____
_____

Lesson 7 Day 1

Date: _____

Spatial Organization, Comparing Objects, and Comparing Characters

Spatial organization explains how things are physically located when compared to other things. If you were to sit in an automobile and look around, what would you see? If another passenger in your car was wearing a blindfold, would you be able to verbally explain to them what the car looks like?

Do you think the below paragraph does a good job of explaining what the inside of the car might look like?

> The car has a steering wheel and a seat for the driver. The interior also has a radio and multiple gauges for fuel level, oil pressure, and water temperature. There are also controls to operate the heating and air conditioning systems. There are sun visors that help keep the sun out of passengers' eyes on a bright sunny day.

Does the above paragraph give the blindfolded person a good visual image of the car's interior? Does the blindfolded person know which side of the car the steering wheel is located? Does the blindfolded person know where the gauges are located and what their shapes might be? Where is the radio located?

Is there any way to make the above paragraph paint a better visual image for the blindfolded passenger? Yes, we could have used spatial organization transitional words to provide the passenger with a better visual image.

Spatial organization transitional words are used to position one object by referring to another object. The table on the next page contains a small sample of spatial organization transitional words and phrases. Almost any word that can be used to tell where an object is located compared to something else can be used as a spatial organization transitional word. These words can also be used together (with each other) to form spatial organization transitional words.

above	before	parallel to	here	nearby	other side of
through	on	onto	around	up	outside of
across	below	behind	in	next to	there
adjacent to	beneath	beyond	inside	close to	to the left of
among	beside	by	into	opposite	to the right of
at that point	between	down	near	over	under
against	on top of	underneath	in between	attached to	to the side of

We will now attempt to provide a better visual image of the previous paragraph by adding appropriate spatial organization transitional words.

 On the left side of the car you will find a steering wheel and a seat for the driver. Slightly above and to the left of the steering wheel there are three round gauges placed in a row. From left to right above each gauge there are words that read fuel level, oil pressure, and water temperature. Right beneath the radio there is an oval shaped pod that houses controls to operate the heating and air conditioning systems. At the top of the windshield, inside the passenger compartment, there are sun visors on swivels that can flip down to help keep the sun out of passengers' eyes on a bright sunny day.

Of course this paragraph is a bit longer than the first paragraph that does not include spatial organization transitional words, but it clearly does a better job of giving the blindfolded passenger an understanding of the layout of the car.

A. Go back and underline the spatial organization transitional words in the previous paragraph.

Lesson 7 Day 2

Spatial Organization, Comparing Objects, and Comparing Characters

Date: _____

A. Answer the questions below with the spatial organization transitional words from the table from Day 1, or use your own words. Use each spatial organization transitional word only once.

1. Bob laid his car keys _____ the table.

2. Darren stood _____ the piano as his sister played a song.

3. Ally was _____ her purring cat.

4. We could hear the people _____ the wall.

5. The new garage is _____ our house.

6. The storm blew _____ our town.

7. Sally sat _____ the famous movie star.

8. They live _____ town.

9. _____ us was a red car with a loud stereo.

10. The roller coaster soared high _____ the rest of the rides.

11. The dart landed _____ the bull's eye.

12. The hot air balloon soared _____ the crowd.

13. Someone placed the soda _____ the milk in the refrigerator.

14. We had to walk _____ Grandpa's house.

15. Lyle lived down the street _____ the railroad tracks.

Level 7, Lesson 7 – Spatial Organization, Comparing Objects, and Comparing Characters

Lesson 7 Day 3

Spatial Organization, Comparing Objects, and Comparing Characters

Date: _____

A. Read the following paragraph. You will notice that it does not contain any spatial organization transitional words. Rewrite this paragraph and add your own spatial organization transitional words. It is fine to modify this paragraph as needed.

I just got a new aquarium for my birthday. The aquarium came with several fish toys, some plastic plants, a heater, a bubbler, and a water filter. I wanted to make the tank fun for the fish, so I began spreading some colorful rocks. Then I inserted the plastic plants. After that, I positioned the bubbler. Next, I installed the heater and water filter. Finally, I placed the fish toys where I wanted them.

_____
_____
_____
_____
_____
_____
_____
_____
_____
_____
_____
_____
_____
_____
_____
_____
_____
_____

Lesson 7 Day 4

Date: _____

Spatial Organization, Comparing Objects, and Comparing Characters

There are two ways to organize a writing that compares two or more objects. The first way is called a **whole-to-whole comparison**. When performing a whole-to-whole comparison, the writer first says all he wants about the first object being compared, and then he does the same, one at a time, for each remaining object to be compared.

If we compared two types of roller coasters, our writing might look like this:

> A steel track roller coaster is a modern day invention. A steel track roller coaster typically provides a very smooth ride. With modern computerized bending machines, the track pattern of a steel roller coaster is limited only by safety concerns and the designer's imagination. Because the wheels of a steel roller coaster hug the inside, top, and bottom of each rail, a steel roller coaster can perform loops, corkscrews, and other gravity defying maneuvers. Because of its design, a steel track roller coaster is somewhat inexpensive to build. A steel track roller coaster can also be premade at the factory and can be installed rather quickly. Wooden roller coasters have been around since the early nineteen hundreds. A wooden roller coaster typically provides a rough ride that is appreciated only by loyal wooden roller coaster enthusiasts. Wooden roller coasters are made of wood so there are some limitations to the height of the track and the maneuvers they are capable of performing. The wheels of older wooden roller coasters typically hug only the top and bottom of the track. Because wooden roller coasters are made from wood, they must be built on-site and are very time consuming and very expensive to build.

It is very easy to see that the writer of the above paragraph first said all he wanted to say about steel track roller coasters and then wooden roller coasters.

The second way to compare two or more objects is called a **part-to-part comparison**. With this type of comparison, the writer compares a single characteristic or feature at a time for all objects being compared. If we were performing a part-to-part comparison, our writing would look as follows:

> A steel track roller coaster is a modern day invention. Wooden roller coasters have been around since the early nineteen hundreds. A steel track roller coaster typically provides a very smooth ride. A wooden roller coaster relies on a bumpy ride to thrill its riders. With modern computerized bending machines, the track patterns of steel roller coasters are limited only by safety concerns and the designer's imagination. Wooden roller coasters are much more limited in height and design due to the inherent structural weakness of wood. Because the wheels of a steel roller coaster hug the inside, top, and bottom of each rail, a steel track roller coaster can perform loops, corkscrews, and other gravity defying maneuvers. Because the wheels of older wooden roller coasters typically hug only the top and bottom of the track, they are limited in the maneuvers they can perform. Because of its design, a steel track roller coaster is somewhat inexpensive to build. A steel track roller coaster can also be premade at the factory and installed rather quickly. Because wooden roller coasters are made from wood, they must be built on-site and are very time consuming and very expensive to build.

A. Write **a part-to-part comparison** between a **swimming pool** and the **ocean**.

_____
_____
_____
_____
_____
_____
_____

Lesson 7 Day 5

Date: _____

Spatial Organization, Comparing Objects, and Comparing Characters

During Day 4 of this lesson we learned how to compare objects by using whole-to-whole or part-to-part comparisons. The very same methods can be used to compare **characters** from a book or a performance (movie, play, opera, etc.). Sometimes comparing characters from the same or different books or performances can help the reader better understand the book (or performance).

What types of things can you compare about two characters? How do the characters vary in the thoughts they have, their roles in the performance, where they live, how they dress, good traits, bad traits, and so on? Anywhere the two characters have similarities or differences are appropriate for comparison.

A. Think of **two characters you have read about or have seen in a performance such as a movie or play**. Write a one paragraph **whole-to-whole** comparison between the two characters.

_____
_____
_____
_____
_____
_____
_____
_____
_____
_____
_____
_____
_____
_____

Level 7, Lesson 7 – Spatial Organization, Comparing Objects, and Comparing Characters

Lesson 8 Day 1

Simile, Metaphor, Analogy, Personification, and Allusion

Date: _____

Using **similes** and **metaphors** in your writing is a fun and exciting way to make your writings more interesting. What are **similes** and **metaphors**?

Let's start by explaining a **simile**. A simile takes an ordinary item and likens it to something else that is extreme or unrealistic. A simile is usually made to prove a point or used simply for effect (to shock the reader). A simile is not actually a true comparison between two things (because one of the comparing items is extreme or unrealistic). You can usually tell if a **simile** is present in a sentence when you see the words **as** or **like**.

<u>Jeremy</u> rolled **like** a <u>log</u> when he fell down the hill.
Her <u>eyes</u> were as blue **as** the <u>ocean</u>.
The boxer's <u>jaw</u> was as tough **as** <u>granite</u>.

You can see that a simile is really only made for effect or to prove a point. Obviously the boxer does not have a jaw that is as tough as granite. Instead, the writer makes this simile simply to express his opinion that the boxer can take a hard punch without being injured.

A **metaphor** is similar to a simile in that it **usually** uses an extreme or unrealistic thing to rename something more ordinary. However, metaphors and similes differ. Instead of saying that one thing is **like** something else (a simile), a **metaphor** actually transforms one thing into something extreme or unrealistic by **renaming** it.

Simile: Jackie was **like** a rabbit as she ran around the track.
Metaphor: Jackie **was** a rabbit as she ran around the track.

Level 7, Lesson 8 – Simile, Metaphor, Analogy, Personification, and Allusion

Can you see the difference? A metaphor can sometimes use words like **is**, **are**, **was**, or **were** (and other words) to signal that a metaphor is coming. However, a metaphor **never** uses the words **like** or **as** to compare.

The <u>water</u> was an <u>ocean</u> pouring from the broken pipe.
<u>Bart</u> is a <u>hero</u>.
Those <u>stairs</u> are <u>mountains</u>.

You can see in this set of examples that the first underlined word is actually renamed by the second underlined word. The bolded words are used to demonstrate that the second underlined word **is** something else.

A. Below are sentences that contain **similes** and **metaphors**. Underline the two words in each sentence that are being compared. Write <u>**M**</u> on the line if the sentence contains a metaphor or <u>**S**</u> for simile.

1. ___ The leopard's spots are as dark as coal.

2. ___ The rain became razors as it hit my skin.

3. ___ Trains are wings for mass transportation.

4. ___ Barbara looked like a leopard in her spotted coat.

5. ___ Jane was the queen of the house.

6. ___ Mike is a tiger when he wrestles for his team.

7. ___ Jordan is like a rocket when he swims.

8. ___ Mary was the cloud that hung over the party.

9. ___ Jessica was as tough as nails as she led the group.

10. ___ Andy was a shark as he bartered for the new car.

11. ___ Julie was like a tornado as she cleaned the house.

12. ___ Farrell acted like the boss of the project.

Level 7, Lesson 8 – Simile, Metaphor, Analogy, Personification, and Allusion

Lesson 8 Day 2

Date: _____

Simile, Metaphor, Analogy, Personification, and Allusion

A. Below are several sentences. If a **metaphor** is present, rewrite the sentence with a **simile** to take its place. If a **simile** is present, rewrite the sentence with a **metaphor** to take its place. It is permissible to modify the sentences to accommodate the new metaphor or simile.

1. Candy was a chicken when she had to carve the turkey.

   _____

2. Betty was a baby when she did not get her way.

   _____

3. The bird was a stone when it dove toward the ground.

   _____

4. Kendra stomped across the floor like an elephant.

   _____

5. A warm bath is like a gentle hug.

   _____

6. That picture is life since it depicts events from long ago.

   _____

7. The horses were like smoke as we tried to catch them.

   _____

8. Our yard was a jungle after letting it grow for three weeks.

   _____

9. Brandon was a vice as he held the newborn calf still.

   _____

Level 7, Lesson 8 – Simile, Metaphor, Analogy, Personification, and Allusion

Lesson 8 Day 3

Simile, Metaphor, Analogy, Personification, and Allusion

Date: _____

Analogies can be very fun to think of and use. Analogies use something extreme, simple, or familiar to explain something that is complicated, unfamiliar, or difficult to explain.

The extreme, simple, or familiar thing used to explain the complicated thing must be somewhat similar to the complicated thing.

Rebuilding the motor in this car was like shocking it back to life.

In this example, instead of trying to explain how a rebuilt motor makes a vehicle operable once again, the writer simply makes the analogy that rebuilding the motor will give it new life.

You might be thinking that an analogy and a simile sound like they do the same thing. Although both are structured in a similar manner, a simile is usually made for artistic or shock value. On the other hand, an analogy is usually made for the purpose of quickly explaining something that is complicated.

Example: (simile)   His boat was like mansion.

Example: (analogy) Changing the flat tire was like putting a new shoe on the car.

A. Write an **S** for **simile** or an **A** for **analogy** on the lines below to identify each sentence.

1. ___ Electricity flowing through a circuit is like water flowing through a pipe.

2. ___ That boy jumped like a cat when he was startled.

3. ___ Fixing the shattered window was like assembling a three dimensional puzzle.

4. ___ The human skeletal system is like the steel frame of a building.

5. ___ Stewart was dancing around like a pinball machine.

6. ___ Henry mixed the chemical formula like a chef makes a cake.

7. ___ Penny is like a robot as she delivers her lines in the play.

8. ___ The ship was like a piece of popcorn as it bounced around the sea.

Level 7, Lesson 8 – Simile, Metaphor, Analogy, Personification, and Allusion

Lesson 8 Day 4

Simile, Metaphor, Analogy, Personification, and Allusion

Date: _____

Personification is the act of giving non-living things human characteristics.

Here is a short paragraph that shows personification of a tent.

   The old tent stood alone in the field. It protected us from the elements and coddled us from the cold. The old tent whistles when the wind blows. The tent has been like an old friend keeping us company on camping trips for many years.

A. Underline all words and phrases that make the tent seem human.

B. Finish the sentences below with your own examples of personification.

1. The old furnace <u>grumbled</u> as it heated our home.

2. The chair _____ as Bob sat down.

3. The tree _____ the sunshine.

4. The old book _____ as it opened.

5. The steam engine _____ black smoke.

6. The storms _____ over night.

7. The tornado went _____ along the coast.

8. The clouds _____ across the sky.

9. The sun _____ upon the swimmers.

10. Annual floods _____ us to be careful.

Level 7, Lesson 8 – Similes, Metaphors, Analogy, and Personification

Lesson 8 Day 5

Simile, Metaphor, Analogy, Personification, and Allusion

Date: _____

Allusion is a reference to a famous person, event of life, or literature. An allusion is a literary device that stimulates the reader's mind by using a well-known reference. Of course for an allusion to be effective the reader must understand the reference being made.

If I take Joe's hat, it could turn into a feud like the one between the Smiths and Jones.

Does this sentence make a good allusion? The answer is **no** because nobody has ever heard of the feud between the Smiths and Jones.

If I take Joe's hat, it could turn into a feud like the one between the Hatfields and McCoys.

This sentence contains a proper allusion, because many people have heard of the famous feud between the Hatfields and McCoys.

An **allusion** can be helpful by drawing upon fame or history to make your writing more interesting. It can also be used to break up the monotony of an otherwise limiting topic for some writings.

A. Write an **X** next to those sentences below that have proper allusions.

1. _____ Devin is weak; he's no Popeye, that is for sure.
2. _____ Tracie is as pretty as the Mona Lisa.
3. _____ If you disagree with Ted it could start a fight like the one between Bob and Michael last week.
4. _____ He was a little wild; I guess you say he was gone with the wind.
5. _____ Even Humpty Dumpty would have trouble putting this mess back together.
6. _____ That software was as slow as my sister Sam.
7. _____ His advice was as sound as Sears.
8. _____ Even Napoleon felt tall once in a while.
9. _____ If you steal his parking place it will start World War II all over again.
10. _____ You'll be as happy as your Aunt Cathy if you win that prize.

Level 7, Lesson 8 – Similes, Metaphors, Analogy, and Personification

Lesson 9 Day 1

Date: _____

Alliteration, Onomatopoeia, Hyperbole, and Oxymoron

Alliteration is the use of two words that begin with the **same consonant** sound that are placed together to make an emphasis.

Example: He was a <u>d</u>apper <u>D</u>an.

Example: We danced the <u>T</u>exas <u>t</u>ango in front of the crowd.

Alliteration is meant to call the attention of the reader by using subtle emphasis. Alliteration can also be used as art in a creative writing to paint a mental picture in the reader's mind.

A. Underline the alliterations contained in the sentences below. (Some have more than one pair.)

1. The silly scorpion kept stinging itself.
2. The cautious camel searched for a wonderful water fountain.
3. The bad boy would not behave in school.
4. Her stunning shoes were so bright and shiny.
5. The cozy couch was a nice change.
6. Our dainty dog Chipper was protecting us.
7. The pleasing picture was up for auction.
8. Our dandy deck was finally finished.
9. The perfect pecan pie was delicious.
10. The green grasshopper sat beneath the window.

Lesson 9 Day 2

Date: _____

Alliteration, Onomatopoeia, Hyperbole, and Oxymoron

Onomatopoeias are words that are pronounced much like the sound they represent. The pronunciation of the word and the connection to the actual sound it represents sometimes take a little bit of imagination.

> **Example**: The <u>bang</u> of the hammer woke us up.
>
> **Example**: The <u>zap</u> of the laser scared us.
>
> **Example**: The constant <u>grinding</u> of her teeth was difficult to listen to.

Below is a table that contains examples of onomatopoeias.

squeal	grinding	click	slam	mangle
buzz	snip	bang	pow	zap
squeak	roaring	grinding	screech	fizz
rattle	pop	whirr	crunch	roar

A. Use the words in the above table (or others you can think of) to write sentences with **onomatopoeias**.

1. _____

   _____

   _____

   _____

   _____

2. _____

   _____

   _____

   _____

   _____

Level 7, Lesson 9 – Alliteration, Onomatopoeia, Hyperbole, and Oxymoron

3. _____

4. _____

5. _____

Lesson 9 Day 3

Date: _____

Alliteration, Onomatopoeia, Hyperbole, and Oxymoron

A **hyperbole** is a **deliberate** exaggeration of something purely for effect or emphasis. It is important for the reader to understand that the hyperbole is intended as an exaggeration. A hyperbole can sometimes emphasize a point without using an exclamation mark at the end of the sentence. Hyperboles should be used sparingly.

> **Example**: We have driven by this house **a thousand times**.
> **Example**: He must have put **a pound of butter** in that cake.
> **Example**: The mountains look **higher than the sky**.

A. Sentences containing a **hyperbole** are fun to write because you can be silly and outrageous. Write five sentences below that contain hyperboles.

1. _____
   _____
   _____
   _____
   _____

2. _____
   _____
   _____
   _____
   _____

Level 7, Lesson 9 – Alliteration, Onomatopoeia, Hyperbole, and Oxymoron

3. _____
   _____
   _____
   _____
   _____

4. _____
   _____
   _____
   _____
   _____

5. _____
   _____
   _____
   _____
   _____

Lesson 9 Day 4

Date: _____

Alliteration, Onomatopoeia, Hyperbole, and Oxymoron

An **oxymoron** is a paradox (self contradictory, illogical) made up of two words. Usually an oxymoron is made from an adjective-noun (crazy professor) or an adverb-adjective (barely full).

definite maybe	original copies	deafening silence	rolling stop	light truck
larger half	plastic glasses	clearly confused	genuine imitation	liquid gas
minor crisis	jumbo shrimp	unbiased opinion	freezer burn	seriously funny
exact estimate	found missing	same difference	giant ant	alone together

A. Write five sentences below using an **oxymoron** from the box above. Of course you can use your own oxymoron as well.

1. _____

2. _____

Level 7, Lesson 9 – Alliteration, Onomatopoeia, Hyperbole, and Oxymoron

3. _____

4. _____

5. _____

Lesson 9 Day 5

Alliteration, Onomatopoeia, Hyperbole, and Oxymoron

Date: _____

A. Write on each line whether the sentence contains an **alliteration, onomatopoeia, hyperbole,** or **oxymoron**.

1. _____ There must have been a thousand birds in the tree.

2. _____ The steel wool was very rough.

3. _____ It was a disorganized plan.

4. _____ It was a cost savings to buy two items instead of one.

5. _____ The proud parents stood over the baby's crib.

6. _____ The car screeched its tires.

7. _____ The barber trimmed my hair with a snip of the scissors.

8. _____ The delayed dinner was worth the wait.

9. _____ That old refrigerator must have weighed a ton.

10. _____ The squeaky mouse ran across the floor.

11. _____ This coffee must have been sitting for a week.

12. _____ This delicious doughnut was just what I needed.

13. _____ The fast snail still finished the race in last place.

14. _____ Her meager wealth was actually very sizable.

15. _____ Dad's tie had a solid mixture of color and stripes.

Level 7, Lesson 9 – Alliteration, Onomatopoeia, Hyperbole, and Oxymoron

Lesson 10 Day 1

Date: _____

Descriptive Writing

In this lesson you will write a **descriptive writing** that is **six** paragraphs in length. A descriptive writing tells about a person, place, or thing. The goal of a good **descriptive writing** is to involve the reader in the **story** as much as possible. You want the reader to feel like they were actually there during the events of the story.

One way to involve a reader in a story is to use adjectives that describe our senses. Boring verbs, boring adjectives, and non-exact nouns have no place in descriptive writing. Here the writer is trying to paint a vivid picture of the person, place, or thing he is trying to describe. It is not enough to tell the reader that an eagle soars (for example); the writer must go into vivid detail about what makes the gliding of an eagle across the sky such a beautiful thing to see. To accomplish this detailed description, the writer typically uses time order words, strong verbs, colorful adjectives, exact nouns, metaphors, similes, analogies, personification, hyperbole, oxymoron, alliteration, or onomatopoeia.

Develop and write a descriptive writing using the following two processes:

Outlining Process
   A. Complete the rough outline
   B. Complete the final outline

Drafting Process
   A. Complete the rough draft
   B. Edit the rough draft
   C. Complete the final draft

Level 7, Lesson 9 – Alliteration, Onomatopoeia, Hyperbole, and Oxymoron

Outlining Process

We will now begin writing your descriptive assignment with the outlining process. Outlining is the process where information about the writing is gathered in order to complete the rough outline and a final outline.

Choose a main topic. Write about one of the following:
- your favorite restaurant
- an item left too long in the refrigerator
- a favorite photograph

Choose your main topic and write it in the main topic section of the rough outline on the next page.

The entire outlining process is explained in **Appendix B**. If you need help in completing the rough outline or the final outline, use Appendix B. Whether or not you use Appendix B first, you still need to complete the rough outline found on the next page and the final outline found in the lesson for Day 2.

Complete the rough outline

Rough Outline

Main Topic:

_____

_____

_____

Subtopic #1: _____

    Details: _____

    _____

    _____

Subtopic #2: _____

    Details: _____

    _____

    _____

Subtopic #3: _____

    Details: _____

    _____

    _____

Subtopic #4: _____

    Details: _____

    _____

    _____

(Lesson 10 Day 2)

Date: _____

Descriptive Writing

Complete the final outline

Final Outline

Introductory Paragraph:

_____
_____
_____
_____
_____

Subtopic 1#:

  Topic Sentence:

_____
_____
_____
_____

  Detail Sentences:

_____
_____
_____
_____
_____
_____
_____

Ending Sentence: (written after the topic sentence and detail sentences)

_____
_____
_____

Subtopic 2#:

    Topic Sentence:

_____
_____
_____
_____

    Detail Sentences:

_____
_____
_____
_____
_____
_____
_____

    Ending Sentence: (written after the topic sentence and detail sentences)

_____
_____
_____

Subtopic 3#:

    Topic Sentence:

_____
_____
_____
_____

    Detail Sentences:

_____
_____
_____
_____
_____
_____
_____
_____

    Ending Sentence: (written after the topic sentence and detail sentences)

_____
_____
_____
_____

Subtopic 4#:

    Topic Sentence:

_____
_____
_____
_____

Detail Sentences:

_____
_____
_____
_____
_____
_____
_____

Ending Sentence: (written after the topic sentence and detail sentences)

_____
_____
_____

Concluding Paragraph:

_____
_____
_____
_____

Lesson 10 Day 3

Date: _____

Descriptive Writing

Drafting Process

<u>Complete the rough draft</u>

So far you have spent quite a bit of time filling out the rough outline and the final outline. As a result, your final outline has all of the necessary pieces to complete your writing.

If you think of something you want to add while you are writing your rough draft, please do so. The final outline will now be used as a guide to write a rough draft.

Start by writing your **introductory paragraph**, sentences for each **subtopic** (topic sentence, detail sentences, and ending sentence), and **concluding paragraph** on the lines below.

_____
_____
_____
_____
_____
_____
_____
_____
_____
_____
_____
_____
_____
_____
_____
_____
_____

Lesson 10 Day 4

Date: _____

Descriptive Writing

<u>Edit the rough draft</u>

It is now time to **edit** the rough draft you wrote on Day 3. Use the editing marks shown in **Appendix C** to correct any mistakes.

Do your paragraphs say what you want them to say? Do the words you chose make sense?

Look for and fix the following errors: 1) incorrectly used, misspelled, or misplaced words, 2) incorrect or missing spacing, 3) incorrect, missing, or misplaced punctuation, and 4) incorrect or missing capitalization.

Lesson 10 Day 5

Date: _____

Descriptive Writing

<u>Complete the final draft</u>

On Day 4 you edited your paragraph. Today you will rewrite your paragraph in its final draft form.

Read your paragraphs one more time. Do your sentences flow well from one to the other? Does your entire writing make sense? Can you make it even better by adding 1) **time order words**, 2) **strong verbs**, 3) **adverbs**, 4) **exact nouns**, 5) **descriptive adjectives**, 6) **metaphors**, 7) **similes**, 8) **analogies**, 9) **personification**, 10) **hyperboles**, 11) **oxymoron**, 12) **alliteration**, and 13) **onomatopoeias**? Rewrite your edited paragraphs below.

_____
_____
_____
_____
_____
_____
_____
_____
_____
_____
_____
_____
_____
_____
_____
_____
_____
_____

Level 7, Lesson 10 – Descriptive Writing

(Lesson 11 Day 1)

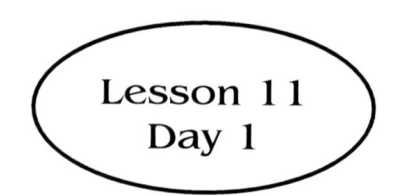

Date: _____

Descriptive Writing

A. Write another **descriptive writing** that is **six** paragraphs in length.

Use the following two processes:

Outlining Process
    A. Complete the rough outline
    B. Complete the final outline

Drafting Process
    A. Complete the rough draft
    B. Edit the rough draft
    C. Complete the final draft

Outlining Process

We will now begin writing your descriptive writing assignment with the outlining process. Outlining is the process where information about the writing is gathered in order to complete the rough outline and a final outline.

The entire outlining process is explained in **Appendix B**. If you need help in completing the rough outline or the final outline, use Appendix B. Whether or not you use Appendix B first, you still need to complete the rough outline and the final outline.

Choose a main topic. Write about one of the following:

- your favorite movie
- the best gift you have ever received
- your favorite place to relax

Choose your main topic and write it in the main topic section of the rough outline found on the next page.

Complete the rough outline

Rough Outline

Main Topic: _____

_____

_____

_____

Subtopic #1: _____

    Details: _____

    _____

    _____

Subtopic #2: _____

    Details: _____

    _____

    _____

Subtopic #3: _____

    Details: _____

    _____

    _____

Subtopic #4: _____

    Details: _____

    _____

    _____

Lesson 11 Day 2

Date: _____

Descriptive Writing

Complete the final outline

Final Outline

Introductory Paragraph:

_____
_____
_____
_____
_____

Subtopic #1:

    Topic Sentence:

    _____
    _____
    _____
    _____

    Detail Sentences:

    _____
    _____
    _____
    _____
    _____
    _____
    _____
    _____

Ending Sentence: (written after the topic sentence and detail sentences)

_____
_____
_____

Subtopic #2:

Topic Sentence:

_____
_____
_____
_____

Detail Sentences:

_____
_____
_____
_____
_____
_____
_____
_____

Ending Sentence: (written after the topic sentence and detail sentences)

_____
_____
_____
_____

Level 7, Lesson 11 – Descriptive Writing

Subtopic #3:

    Topic Sentence:

_____

_____

_____

_____

    Detail Sentences:

_____

_____

_____

_____

_____

_____

_____

_____

    Ending Sentence: (written after the topic sentence and detail sentences)

_____

_____

_____

_____

Subtopic #4:

    Topic Sentence:

_____

_____

_____

Detail Sentences:

_____
_____
_____
_____
_____
_____
_____
_____

Ending Sentence: (written after the topic sentence and detail sentences)

_____
_____
_____
_____

Concluding Paragraph:

_____
_____
_____
_____
_____

Lesson 11 Day 3

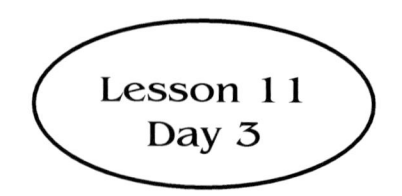

Date: _____

Descriptive Writing

Drafting Process

Complete the rough draft

So far you have spent quite a bit of time filling out the rough outline and the final outline. As a result, your final outline has all of the necessary pieces to complete your writing.

If you think of something you want to add while you are writing your rough draft, please do so. The final outline will now be used as a guide to write a rough draft.

Start by writing your **introductory paragraph**, sentences for each **subtopic** (topic sentence, detail sentences, and ending sentence), and **concluding paragraph** on the lines below.

_____
_____
_____
_____
_____
_____
_____
_____
_____
_____
_____
_____
_____
_____

Lesson 11 Day 4

Descriptive Writing

Date: _____

Edit the rough draft

It is now time to **edit** the rough draft you wrote on Day 3. Use the editing marks shown in **Appendix C** to correct any mistakes.

Do your paragraphs say what you want them to say? Do the words you chose make sense?

Look for and fix the following errors: 1) incorrectly used, misspelled, or misplaced words, 2) incorrect or missing spacing, 3) incorrect, missing, or misplaced punctuation, and 4) incorrect or missing capitalization.

Lesson 11 Day 5

Descriptive Writing

Date: _____

<u>Complete the final draft</u>

On Day 4 you edited your paragraphs. Today you will rewrite your paragraphs in their final draft form.

Read your paragraphs one more time. Do your sentences flow well from one to the other? Does your entire writing make sense? Can you make it even better by adding 1) **time order words**, 2) **strong verbs**, 3) **adverbs**, 4) **exact nouns**, 5) **descriptive adjectives**, 6) **metaphors**, 7) **similes**, 8) **analogies**, 9) **personification**, 10) **hyperbole**, 11) **oxymoron**, 12) **alliteration**, or 13) **onomatopoeia**? Rewrite your edited paragraphs below.

_____
_____
_____
_____
_____
_____
_____
_____
_____
_____
_____
_____
_____
_____
_____
_____

Level 7, Lesson 11 – Descriptive Writing

Lesson 12 Review Day 1

Date: _____

Review of Spatial Organization

above	before	parallel to	here	nearby	other side of
through	on	onto	around	up	outside of
across	below	behind	in	next to	there
adjacent to	beneath	beyond	inside	close to	to the left of
among	beside	by	into	opposite	to the right of
at that point	between	down	near	over	under
against	on top of	underneath	in between	attached to	to the side of

A. Finish the sentences below with **spatial organization transitional** words from the table above, or you can use your own words. Use each spatial organization transitional word only once.

1. Our favorite restaurant was _____ the car wash.

2. Bailey stood _____ the two arguing children.

3. I slid the clean pan _____ the other clean pans.

4. Sheila parked her bike _____ the water fountain.

5. Mom placed my chair _____ the couch.

6. The group had a meeting _____.

7. The ceiling fan spun _____ our heads.

8. Put the groceries _____ the chair.

9. Crystal sat _____ me in the car.

10. Dad placed the fresh eggs _____ the frying pan.

11. The rock landed _____ my feet.

12. The car whizzed _____ our car.

13. Susan placed the cookies _____ the counter.

14. The Smiths lived _____ the Jones' residence.

15. Doug lives _____ us.

Level 7, Lesson 12 - Review of Lessons 7-11

Lesson 12 Review Day 2

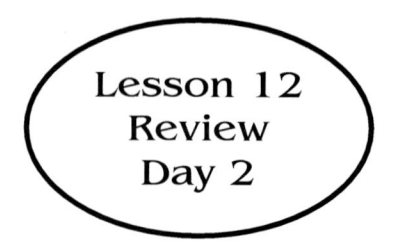

Review of Simile, Metaphor, Analogy, Personification, and Allusion

A. Write on each line whether the sentence contains a **simile**, **metaphor**, **analogy**, or **personification**.

1. _____ Carrie twirled like a top as she danced.

2. _____ The branches danced in the storm.

3. _____ The scissors cut through the material like a hot knife through butter.

4. _____ Flowers are life to those feeling sad.

5. _____ The wind spoke to us as it blew across the prairie.

6. _____ Cassie's love of chocolate was her Achilles' heel.

7. _____ The door screams every time it is opened.

8. _____ The tractor awoke from a long sleep.

9. _____ The golf club became an extension of Glenn's arm.

10. _____ My feet were like rocks after standing on them all day.

11. _____ The geyser belches steam into the sky everyday.

12. _____ I am afraid of spiders, but I'm no cowardly lion.

13. _____ The piece of paper was a bird as it flew through the sky.

14. _____ The sky wept with a torrential rain.

15. _____ Diagnosing an illness is like investigating a crime.

Level 7, Lesson 12 - Review of Lessons 7-11

Lesson 12 Review Day 3

Review of Alliteration, Onomatopoeia, Hyperbole, and Oxymoron

Date: _____

A. Write on each line whether the sentence contains an **alliteration, onomatopoeia, hyperbole,** or **oxymoron**.

1. _____ The pop of the cork was loud.

2. _____ The slow jet made the trip in two hours.

3. _____ Carol's colorful car was fun to drive.

4. _____ The tornado roared through the town.

5. _____ The crazy clown made us all laugh.

6. _____ The dried leaves crackled as we walked across them.

7. _____ Her glasses weighed a ton.

8. _____ The solution to the puzzle was deceptively simple.

9. _____ The fancy farmer planted some colorful gourds.

10. _____ We waited an eternity in that line.

11. _____ I called that number a thousand times.

12. _____ Allen considered himself an army of one.

13. _____ The car's engine popped as it drove past us.

14. _____ The new car was a driving delight.

15. _____ There must be a million dirty glasses in this sink.

Level 7, Lesson 12 - Review of Lessons 7-11

Lesson 12 Review Day 4

Date: _____

| Review of Descriptive Writing |

A. In this exercise you will write a **one** paragraph descriptive writing about **an animal you might see in the ocean**. Conduct some **outlining** by completing the rough outline and final outline below.

Rough Outline

Main Topic:

_____
_____
_____

Details: (used to make detail sentences)

_____
_____
_____
_____
_____
_____
_____
_____
_____
_____

Level 7, Lesson 12 - Review of Lessons 7-11

Final Outline

Topic Sentence:

_____
_____
_____
_____

Detail Sentences:

_____
_____
_____
_____
_____
_____
_____
_____

Ending Sentence: (written after the topic sentence and detail sentences)

_____
_____
_____

Lesson 12 Review Day 5

Date: _____

Review of Descriptive Writing

A. On Day 4 of this lesson you completed an outline for **an animal you might see in the ocean**. Write a rough draft paragraph using the information from your final outline.

Lesson 13 Day 1

Date: _____

Parts of a Creative Story

For most people, writing a creative story is more enjoyable than writing any other type of story. The author of these types of stories has free reign to be as creative as possible when creating a plot (what happened in the story), characters, and setting (the world in which the story takes place). Creative stories are where many Hollywood screenplays are born.

Writing a creative story is usually easier if the writer first develops the characters, setting, and plot. Until you know who your characters are, where exactly the story takes place, or what happens (plot) during the story, it will be difficult to write a focused story.

After the **plot**, **characters**, and **setting** are developed, they are used along with an outline to focus the writer of the story.

A creative story has three parts, an **introduction**, **body**, and a **conclusion**.
- The **introduction** is located at the beginning of the story. It introduces the **characters** and explains the **setting** in which the story occurs.
- The main part of the story is called the **body**. This part of the story may be the most important since it explains what the story is about and tells what happens next. This is also the part that usually contains the turning point. You will use the information contained in the plot development form, character development form, and setting development form to create the rough outline, the final outline, and the creative story itself. Somewhere in the **body** there is usually a **turning point**. A **turning point** is the part of the plot that is 1) the climax of the story, 2) the part of the story where everything changes, or 3) the part of the story where suddenly everything makes sense.
- The **conclusion** is the part that tells how the story ends.

Level 7, Lesson 13 – Parts of a Creative Story

Develop a six paragraph creative writing by using the following writing process:

Story Process
    A. Develop the plot
    B. Develop the characters
    C. Develop the setting

Outlining Process
    A. Complete the rough outline
    B. Complete the final outline

Drafting Process
    A. Complete the rough draft
    B. Edit the rough draft   → Not covered in this lesson.
    C. Complete the final draft

Story Process

Develop the plot

We will now start our story by developing a plot. We will use the main topic of **a gang of outlaws who are planning on going on a crime spree**. How many outlaws are in this gang? What types of crimes are they planning to attempt? Where and when does this story take place? You can see how the answers to even these basic questions can set the stage for the entire story. In a creative story you decide what happens. It's your chance to explore and be creative.

A. Use the **plot development form** below to write ideas for the plot of your story. Do not try to write a story on this form. The plot development form is only used to get you to think about the main flow of your story. "This happens, then that happens, then this happens, *and so on....*"

Plot Development Form

_____
_____
_____
_____
_____
_____
_____
_____
_____
_____
_____
_____
_____
_____
_____
_____
_____
_____
_____
_____
_____
_____
_____
_____

Lesson 13 Day 2

Parts of a Creative Story

Date: _____

So far you have created a short plot. Now it is time to develop one of the characters in your gang of outlaws.

Develop the characters

To develop a character, what types of things do we need to know? Of course it depends on the story being told, but answering the questions on the character development form on the next page can help this process. Look back at our example of the gang planning to go on a crime spree. Who is the leader? Has he committed a crime before? Has he been in jail before? What does he look like? Is he well-spoken or educated? Does he have a family? You can see how answering these questions, as well as many others, will shape the characteristics that define your character.

Character Development Form

1. What is the character's name? _____

2. Is this character human? _____

3. Is this character a male or female? _____

4. Where is this character from? _____

5. What does this character look like? (height, weight, hair color, physical characteristics)

   _____
   _____
   _____
   _____
   _____

6. Is this character friendly or hostile?

   _____

7. Does this character have any special traits or talents? If so, what are they?

   _____
   _____
   _____
   _____
   _____

8. Does this character have certain views about something that is going to happen in the story? If so, what are they?

   _____
   _____
   _____
   _____
   _____

Level 7, Lesson 13 – Parts of a Creative Story

Lesson 13 Day 3

Parts of a Creative Story

Date: _____

Develop the setting

The setting tells **when** and **where** the story takes place. You can imagine that some stories would not make much sense unless the setting was explained by the author. For example, if you had a story where the characters were talking about how cold they were, it might be helpful to understand that the story takes place somewhere with a severe winter climate.

Is the setting dark, hot, cold, wet, scary, or dangerous? Is it set in a desert, a foreign country, an ocean, a forest, or somewhere in outer space? What does the place look like? Does it have buildings, people, or scenery? All of these descriptions are important to help the reader understand the story.

The setting must also match the plot and characters of your story. For example, it would not make much sense to have a scary story take place in the daytime on a busy street in the middle of a city, because a good scary story usually takes place in the dark in some secluded area.

A. Use the setting development form on the next page to develop the setting for your story about the gang of outlaws.

Setting Development Form

Where does the story take place? _____
_____
_____

In what time period does your story take place? _____
_____
_____

Does the story take place in the daytime or at night? _____
_____
_____

What does it look like where the story takes place? _____
_____
_____
_____
_____
_____
_____
_____

List anything else the reader needs to know about the setting. _____
_____
_____
_____
_____
_____
_____

Lesson 13 Day 4

Parts of a Creative Story

Date: _____

Since you have developed a plot, a character, and a setting, it is time to start the outlining process.

Outlining Process

The entire outlining process is explained in **Appendix B**. If you need help in completing the rough outline or the final outline, use Appendix B. Whether or not you use Appendix B, you still need to complete the rough outline and the final outline on the following pages.

Complete the rough outline

Rough Outline

Main Topic:

_____

_____

_____

Subtopic #1:_____

    Details:_____

    _____

    _____

Subtopic #2:_____

    Details:_____

    _____

    _____

Subtopic #3:_____

    Details:_____

    _____

    _____

Subtopic #4:_____

    Details:_____

    _____

    _____

Level 7, Lesson 13 – Parts of a Creative Story

Complete the final outline

Final Outline

Introductory Paragraph:

_____
_____
_____
_____
_____

Subtopic #1:

   Topic Sentence:

   _____
   _____
   _____
   _____

   Detail Sentences:

   _____
   _____
   _____
   _____
   _____
   _____
   _____
   _____

   Ending Sentence: (written after the topic sentence and detail sentences)

   _____
   _____
   _____

Subtopic #2:

    Topic Sentence:

_____
_____
_____
_____

    Detail Sentences:

_____
_____
_____
_____
_____
_____
_____

    Ending Sentence: (written after the topic sentence and detail sentences)

_____
_____
_____
_____

Subtopic #3:

    Topic Sentence:

_____
_____
_____
_____

Detail Sentences:

_____
_____
_____
_____
_____
_____
_____

Ending Sentence: (written after the topic sentence and detail sentences)

_____
_____
_____

Subtopic #4:

Topic Sentence:

_____
_____
_____

Detail Sentences:

_____
_____
_____
_____
_____
_____
_____

Ending Sentence: (written after the topic sentence and detail sentences)

_____

_____

_____

_____

Concluding Paragraph:

_____

_____

_____

_____

_____

Lesson 13
Day 5

Parts of a Creative Story

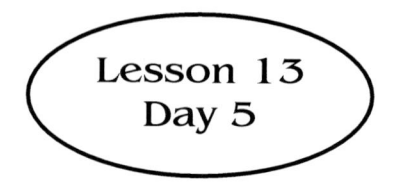

Date: _____

A. Answer the following questions.

1. Can the writer of a creative story create his own plot?

    a. no

    b. yes

2. Can the writer of a creative story create his own characters?

    a. no

    b. yes

3. When should the **plot**, **setting**, and **characters** be **developed**?
    a. They should be developed after the middle portion of the story is written.
    b. They should be developed before the author starts to write the actual story.
    c. They are not really necessary unless you need guidance.
    d. They should be developed after the beginning paragraph is written.

4. Why is a **plot** important?
    a. because it tells how the story ends
    b. because it tells what happens next in the story
    c. because it tells where the story takes place
    d. because it tells who wrote the story

5. Circle the answer that is **not** part of the definition of the turning point.
    a. the climax of the story
    b. the part of the story where everything changes
    c. the end of the story
    d. the part of the story where suddenly everything makes senses

Level 7, Lesson 13 – Parts of a Creative Story

Lesson 14 Day 1

Quotations, Dialogue, Point of View, and Voice

Date: _____

Quotations are used to capture spoken words and place them into a written form. When a person's **exact words** are captured and placed into a writing, a **direct quotation** is used. When we simply summarize another person's words in a sentence, an indirect quotation is used. Since an indirect quotation is **not** the exact words of another person, quotation marks are **not** used we insert them into our writings.

Direct Quotation: Mom said, "I am tired and I want to take a nap."

Indirect Quotation: Mom said that she is tired and wants to take a nap.

Can you see the difference between the two? Here are more examples of indirect quotations.

Danny asked Karen for a ride home.
Amy laughed and said that she liked that joke.
Kristin said that she likes to dance and sing.

A. Read the paragraph below and underline the sentences that contain **indirect quotations**.

Barb and Denise said that they wanted to go to the mall and look for gifts for Todd's birthday. They drove Denise's new car and it broke down on the way there. They called a tow truck and asked the lady on the telephone to send a truck to pick them up. While they were waiting for the tow truck, Denise told Barb that she had already purchased one present for Todd. Once the tow truck arrived, the driver said it would cost fifty dollars to tow the car to the dealership. Dad said that he would pick them up at the dealership. I told Dad I would go with him.

Lesson 14 Day 2

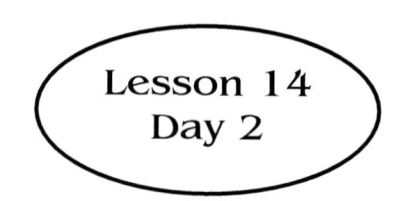

Quotations, Dialogue, Point of View, and Voice

Date: _____

A **direct quotation** is used to capture and write the **actual words spoken by a person**. The first letter of the first word of a direct quotation is capitalized. **Quotation marks** are placed before and after the **exact spoken words** of the speaker.

Michelle said, "It's time to make pie."

As you can see from the above example, whenever a sentence contains a direct quotation, there is also a **speaker tag** located somewhere in the sentence. The speaker tag identifies the speaker of the quoted words.

If the speaker tag comes first in the sentence, place a comma between the **speaker's exact spoken words** and the **speaker tag**. Ending **punctuation** is placed inside the quotation marks.

Phyllis commented, "I think we should all go."

Carrey asked, "Are you the person who sang?"

Darcie said, "I want to paint something."

Sometimes, simply to provide variation within a writing, the writer will place the speaker tag at the **end of the sentence** instead of at the beginning. If the **speaker tag** comes last in a direct quotation, a **comma** (used in place of a period), **question mark**, or **exclamation mark** is placed inside the quotation marks. A period is placed after the speaker tag.

"This car is nice," said Trudy.

"Have you washed your hands?" asked Mom.

"Please stop jumping!" exclaimed Frances.

Level 7, Lesson 14 – Quotations, Dialogue, Point of View, and Voice

A. Below are several sentences that contain **direct** and **indirect quotations**. Rewrite each sentence correctly by adding correct **capitalization** and **punctuation**.

1. I didn't clean my room said Dan

2. Judith asked why didn't you eat your peas

3. is it time to eat asked Jacob

4. can you help me carry this box asked Kim

5. Tina asked can I go to the store with you

6. I dropped another glass of water said Mia

7. that tiger is a fast sprinter said our guide

8. Ben said I am playing basketball this year

Sometimes direct quotations are **divided**, meaning that additional non-quoted language, such as the speaker tag, interrupts the quoted sentence. When this occurs, the **direct quotation** is set apart from the rest of the sentence by **commas** and only one capital letter is required at the beginning of the direct quotation. Use a **lowercase letter** for the second part of the quotation.

"**M**y brother**,**" Jan said**,** "helped me study."

The speaker tag **Jan said** interrupts and divides Jan's direct quotation. The word **helped** starts with a lowercase letter because it is in the second part of the quotation.

"We need to do our homework," Lori said, "or else we will fail."

"Did you arrive," asked Miss Parker, "on time?"

B. Rewrite each quotation below that is not written correctly. Remember to use **quotation marks**, **punctuation**, and **capitalization** where needed in these quotations. If the quotation is already written correctly, simply write the word **correct** on the line.

1. "many of us said Ann are hungry"

   _____

2. "Did you climb the ladder," asked Ed, "to look at the roof?"

   _____

3. "These shoes, said Dad, are wet".

   _____

4. May I asked Mary play in the game?

   _____

5. "That." said the umpire, "was a foul ball."

   _____

Lesson 14 Day 3

Quotations, Dialogue, Point of View, and Voice

Date: _____

Dialogue is nothing more than a collection of **direct quotations** that occur during a conversation between two or more people. When you write dialogue, each time a different person speaks you must start a new paragraph. **Dialogue** should sound like a normal conversation between people. Once the speaker is identified in a paragraph by a speaker tag, another speaker tag is not required again for that same paragraph even if the speaker has additional dialogue in that paragraph. Simply place quotes at the beginning and end of the additional dialogue sentences. For example:

"The bases are loaded," said Ben. "I'll bet Alan hits a home run. He will at least hit a single."

Below is an example of dialogue between two friends.

A. Underline any portion that is written incorrectly.

"How was your weekend, Bill?" asked Ken.

Bill said, I got home from work on Friday and discovered that my refrigerator was broken."

"Was it an old refrigerator?" asked Ken.

"It was only two years old, Bill answered, but we still had to buy a new refrigerator that night.

"Wow, I am sorry to hear that," said Ken.

"Well," said Bill, "right after our new refrigerator was delivered, I plugged it in only to find out that it too was broken."

"That's impossible" said Ken.

"After taking a few deep breaths," said Bill, "my wife suggested that I check the fuse box to make sure we hadn't simply blown a fuse."

Oh, no," said Ken.

"Yes, it turned out to be the most expensive fuse in the world," said Bill. "The worst part was I called the store the next day to try and get our old refrigerator back, but it had already been taken to the dump."

Date: _____

B. Rewrite the previous dialogue in the correct form.

Lesson 14 Day 4

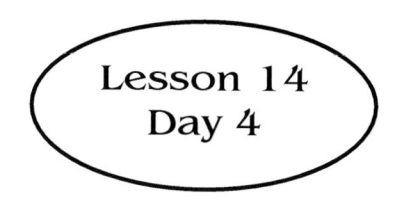

Date: _____

Quotations, Dialogue, Point of View, and Voice

When we tell a story, it can be told from a **first-person** point of view or a **third-person** point of view.

A story told from the first-person point of view is told by someone who was a witness to the event or a character in the story. Stories written in first-person point of view use words like **I**, **me**, **my**, **mine**, **we**, **us**, **our**, and **ours** to tell the story.

When a story is told from a third-person point of view, the person telling the story was not present during the event. When a story is told from a third-person point of view, the story teller (who is actually a narrator) uses words like **he**, **she**, **him**, **her**, **his**, **it**, **its**, **their**, **theirs**, **they**, and **them**.

A. You will now write a short **one** paragraph story, from either the **first-person** or **third-person point of view**, about something you saw first-hand (first-person point of view), or something you read about or heard from a friend (third-person point of view). You will not have to perform any outlining for this lesson.

_____
_____
_____
_____
_____
_____
_____
_____
_____
_____
_____
_____

Level 7, Lesson 14 – Quotations, Dialogue, Point of View, and Voice

Lesson 14 Day 5

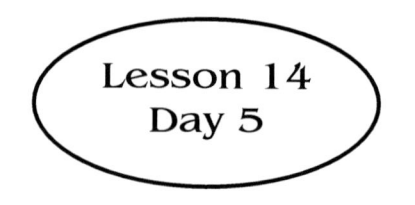

Date: _____

Quotations, Dialogue, Point of View, and Voice

Humans speak to each other by using voices. Obviously, in your lifetime you have heard speakers use many different kinds of voices such as **happy**, **sad**, **excited**, **serious**, **angry**, or somewhere in between. When you write you use a voice, which is expressed in your choice of words and punctuation.

When you write you must constantly keep in mind the **voice** you want to express. Are you in a good mood, angry, or somewhere in between? Who is your audience? Are you writing a letter to a business, or are you writing a quick note to friend?

Typically people match the type of voice they wish to express with a **formal** or **informal** style of writing.

What is the difference between **formal** and **informal writing**? Informal writing is writing that **sounds** more like a casual conversation. A writer using informal language might use slang, funny words, abbreviations, or incomplete sentences. A formal writing style **sounds** formal since it does not use slang, funny words, abbreviations, or incomplete sentences.

If you are in a happy mood and writing a letter to a friend, you would probably write in a **friendly** voice using an **informal** style.

On the other hand, if your audience is a business, then it would probably be a good idea to write in a **serious** voice using a **formal** style.

A. Answer these questions.
 1. What **voice** and **style** would you likely use if you were writing a letter to your grandparents to tell them about the good grades you received?
    a. angry/informal
    b. happy/informal
    c. serious/formal
    d. happy/formal
 2. What kind of writing **voice** would you use if you were writing a letter to your friend with whom you were angry?
    a. formal
    b. informal
    c. happy voice
    d. angry

Level 7, Lesson 14 – Quotations, Dialogue, Point of View, and Voice

3. What **style** of writing would you use if you were writing a letter to a store asking for a refund?

   a. friendly

   b. serious

   c. angry

4. What writing **style** would you likely use if you were writing a quick message to a friend?

   a. formal

   b. informal

   c. thankful

B. Below is an **informal** writing that is written using a happy **voice**. Turn this letter into a **formal** writing using a **serious** voice.

   Hi, Bridgett!

   What's up? I am just sitting here looking at some pics of me and my buds. I think a couple of these were taken at your place. I can tell by the cool painting in the background. Anyway, would you like to catch a flick sometime this weekend? Give me a shout and let me know.

   Cheers,

   Cris

Level 7, Lesson 14 – Quotations, Dialogue, Point of View, and Voice

Lesson 15 Day 1

Date: _____

Creative Writing

In a creative story the author gets to use his creative talents to develop a **plot**, a **setting**, and **characters** for his story. Since the author is primarily using his imagination to construct the entire story, there is usually very little outside research to conduct. Writing a creative story is a lot of fun because the author gets to be creative.

Sometimes it's easier to write a creative story if the plot, setting, and characters are first developed. After the **plot**, **characters**, and **setting** are developed, they are used as an outline to guide and focus the writer of the story.

We will now begin the writing process for a **six** paragraph **creative story**.

Developing and writing a creative story uses the following three processes:

Story Process
  A. Develop the plot
  B. Develop the characters
  C. Develop the setting

Outlining Process
  A. Complete the rough outline
  B. Complete the final outline

Drafting Process
  A. Complete the rough draft
  B. Edit the rough draft
  C. Complete the final draft

During the **outlining process** the plot, characters, setting, rough outline, and final outline are developed. The **drafting process** uses the information gathered during outlining process to complete a rough and final draft of the creative story.

Story Process

As with all stories, a creative story needs to have a **main topic** to provide the author with some very general guidance. For this assignment write a story about a **famous explorer who has found some caves with his friend that have never been explored**.

Think of a **main topic** for this broad idea and write it in the **main topic** section of the rough outline found on Day 2 of this lesson.

Develop the plot

The plot tells what happens in your story. Without a plot, your characters could exist, but they would have nothing to do. A plot tells what happens next, to whom it happens, why it happens, when it happens, and where it happens. The plot is the foundation upon which the entire story is built.

Usually the plot contains a **turning point** somewhere in the story. The turning point is the part of the plot that is the climax of the story, the part of the story where everything changes, or the part of the story when suddenly everything makes sense. Usually things start out slowly in a story and then build up to the turning point.

Sometimes the **characters** or **setting** are developed before the **plot**. It really depends on the preference of the writer.

Use the **plot development form** on the next page to write ideas for the plot of your story. Do not try to write a story on this form. The plot development form is only used to get you to think about the main flow of your story. "This happens, then that happens, then this happens, *and so on....*" Remember, your plot should be related to the main topic you already wrote down on the rough outline.

Plot Development Form

So far you have written a **main topic** on the rough outline and developed a related **plot** on the plot development form. Now it is time to develop **two** characters for your story about a **famous explorer who has found some caves with his friend that have never been explored**.

Develop the characters

What types of things do we need to know to develop a character? It depends on the story being told, but knowing the types of things listed on the character development form usually helps develop a character.

For this exercise you will develop two characters of your choice. Use your imagination and create some ideas to describe the characters. Two character development forms have been provided on the following pages to assist in developing your character.

Character Development Form

1. What is the character's name? _____

2. Is this character human? _____

3. Is this character a male or female? _____

4. Where is this character from? _____

5. What does this character look like? (height, weight, hair color, physical characteristics)

   _____
   _____
   _____
   _____
   _____

6. Is this character friendly or hostile?

   _____

7. Does this character have any special traits or talents? If so, what are they?

   _____
   _____
   _____
   _____

8. Does this character have certain views about something that is going to happen in the story? If so, what are they?

   _____
   _____
   _____
   _____
   _____

Character Development Form

1. What is the character's name? _____

2. Is this character human? _____

3. Is this character a male or female? _____

4. Where is this character from? _____

5. What does this character look like? (height, weight, hair color, physical characteristics)

   _____
   _____
   _____
   _____
   _____

6. Is this character friendly or hostile?

   _____

7. Does this character have any special traits or talents? If so, what are they?

   _____
   _____
   _____
   _____
   _____

8. Does this character have certain views about something that is going to happen in the story? If so, what are they?

   _____
   _____
   _____
   _____
   _____

So far you have written a **main topic** on the rough outline, developed a **plot** on the plot development form, and developed two **characters** on the character development forms. Now it is time to develop a **setting** for your story.

Develop the setting

The setting tells **when** and **where** the story takes place. Describing the setting in great detail will make the story more interesting to the reader by making him feel like he was actually there when the story occurred. Use the setting development form on the next page to describe the setting for your story about a **famous explorer who has found some caves with his friend that have never been explored**.

Setting Development Form

Where does the story take place? _____
_____
_____

In what time period does your story take place? _____
_____
_____

Does the story take place in the daytime or at night? _____
_____
_____

What does it look like where the story takes place? _____
_____
_____
_____
_____
_____
_____
_____

List anything else the reader needs to know about the setting. _____
_____
_____
_____
_____
_____
_____

Lesson 15 Day 2

Creative Writing

Date: _____

You have already developed a plot, two characters, and a setting. You will use the information contained in the plot development form, character development form, and setting development form to create the rough outline, the final outline, and the creative story.

A creative story has the following three parts: an **introduction**, a **body**, and a **conclusion**.

- The **introduction** starts the story. It introduces the **characters** and explains the **setting** in which the story occurs.
- The main part of the story is called the **body**. This part of the story may be the most important since it explains what the story is about and tells what happens next. This is also the part that contains the turning point.
- The **conclusion** is the final part of the story that tells how it ends.

Keep these parts in mind as you fill out the rough outline and the final outline found on the next two pages.

Outlining Process

The entire outlining process is explained in **Appendix B**. If you need help in completing the rough outline or the final outline, use Appendix B. Whether or not you use Appendix B, you still need to complete the rough outline and the final outline on the following pages.

Level 7, Lesson 15 – Creative Writing

Complete the rough outline

Rough Outline

Main Topic:

_____

_____

_____

Subtopic #1: _____

    Details: _____

    _____

    _____

Subtopic #2: _____

    Details: _____

    _____

    _____

Subtopic #3: _____

    Details: _____

    _____

    _____

Subtopic #4: _____

    Details: _____

    _____

    _____

Complete the final outline

Final Outline

Introductory Paragraph:

_____
_____
_____
_____
_____

Subtopic #1:

    Topic Sentence:

    _____
    _____
    _____

    Detail Sentences:

    _____
    _____
    _____
    _____
    _____
    _____
    _____
    _____

Ending Sentence: (written after the topic sentence and detail sentences)

_____
_____
_____

Subtopic #2:

Topic Sentence:

_____
_____
_____
_____

Detail Sentences:

_____
_____
_____
_____
_____
_____
_____

Ending Sentence: (written after the topic sentence and detail sentences)

_____
_____
_____
_____

Subtopic #3:

    Topic Sentence:

_____
_____
_____
_____

    Detail Sentences:

_____
_____
_____
_____
_____
_____
_____

    Ending Sentence: (written after the topic sentence and detail sentences)

_____
_____
_____
_____

Subtopic #4:

    Topic Sentence:

_____
_____
_____
_____

Detail Sentences:

_____
_____
_____
_____
_____
_____
_____
_____

Ending Sentence: (written after the topic sentence and detail sentences)

_____
_____
_____
_____

Concluding Paragraph:

_____
_____
_____
_____
_____

Lesson 15 Day 3		Date: _____

Creative Writing

Drafting Process

<u>Complete the rough draft</u>

So far you have spent quite a bit of time filling out the rough outline and the final outline. As a result, your final outline has all of the necessary pieces to complete your writing.

If you think of something you want to add while you are writing your rough draft, please do so. The final outline will now be used as a guide to write a rough draft.

Start by writing your **introductory paragraph**, sentences for each **subtopic** (topic sentence, detail sentences, and ending sentence), and **concluding paragraph** on the lines below.

_____
_____
_____
_____
_____
_____
_____
_____
_____
_____
_____
_____
_____
_____
_____

Lesson 15 Day 4

Creative Writing

Date: _____

<u>Edit the rough draft</u>

It is now time to **edit** the rough draft you wrote on Day 3. Use the editing marks shown in **Appendix C** to correct any mistakes.

Do your paragraphs say what you want them to say? Do the words you chose make sense?

Look for and fix the following errors: 1) incorrectly used, misspelled, or misplaced words, 2) incorrect or missing spacing, 3) incorrect, missing, or misplaced punctuation, and 4) incorrect or missing capitalization.

Lesson 15 Day 5

Date: _____

Creative Writing

Complete the final draft

On Day 4 you edited your rough draft. Today you will rewrite your story in its final draft form.

Read your story one more time. Do your sentences flow well from one to the other? Does your entire story make sense? Can you make it even better by adding 1) **time order words**, 2) **strong verbs**, 3) **adverbs**, 4) **exact nouns**, 5) **descriptive adjectives**, 6) **metaphors**, 7) **similes**, 8) **analogies**, 9) **personification**, 10) **hyperbole**, 11) **oxymoron**, 12) **alliteration**, or 13) **onomatopoeia**? Rewrite your edited paragraphs below.

_____
_____
_____
_____
_____
_____
_____
_____
_____
_____
_____
_____
_____
_____
_____
_____
_____

Level 7, Lesson 10 – Descriptive Writing

Lesson 16 Day 1

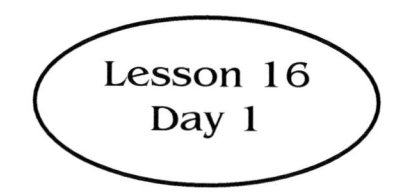

Date: _____

Creative Writing

Develop and write another **six** paragraph **creative story** using the following three processes:

Story Process
  A. Develop the plot
  B. Develop the characters
  C. Develop the setting

Outlining Process
  A. Complete the rough outline
  B. Complete the final outline

Drafting Process
  A. Complete the rough draft
  B. Edit the rough draft
  C. Complete the final draft

Story Process

As with all stories, a creative story needs to have a **main topic** to provide the author with some very general guidance. Use the following sentence as a story starter. Use this sentence to develop your creative story.

"She looked into the room and everything seemed normal, then all of a sudden….."

Develop the plot

The plot tells what happens in your story. Without a plot, your characters could exist, but they would have nothing to do. A plot tells what happens next, to whom it happens, why it happens, when it happens, and where it happens. The plot is the foundation upon which the entire story is built.

Usually the plot contains a **turning point** somewhere in the story. The turning point is the part of the plot that is the climax of the story, the part of the story where everything changes, or the part of the story when suddenly everything makes sense. Usually things start out slowly in a story and then build up to the turning point.

Sometimes the **characters** or **setting** are developed before the **plot**. It really depends on the preference of the writer.

Use the **plot development form** on the next page to write ideas for the plot of your story. Do not try to write a story on this form. The plot development form is only used to get you to think about the main flow of your story. "This happens, then that happens, then this happens, *and so on….*" Remember, your plot should be related to the main topic you already wrote on the rough outline.

Plot Development Form

So far you have written a **main topic** on the rough outline and developed a related **plot** on the plot development form. Now it is time to develop characters for your story.

Develop the characters

For this exercise you will develop two characters of your choice. Use your imagination and create some ideas to describe these characters. Two character development forms have been provided on the next two pages to assist you in developing your characters from the story starter on the first page of this day's lesson.

Character Development Form

1. What is the character's name? _____

2. Is this character human? _____

3. Is this character a male or female? _____

4. Where is this character from? _____

5. What does this character look like? (height, weight, hair color, physical characteristics)

   _____
   _____
   _____
   _____
   _____

6. Is this character friendly or hostile?

   _____

7. Does this character have any special traits or talents? If so, what are they?

   _____
   _____
   _____
   _____
   _____

8. Does this character have certain views about something that is going to happen in the story? If so, what are they?

   _____
   _____
   _____
   _____
   _____

Level 7, Lesson 16 – Creative Writing

Character Development Form

1. What is the character's name? _____

2. Is this character human? _____

3. Is this character a male or female? _____

4. Where is this character from? _____

5. What does this character look like? (height, weight, hair color, physical characteristics)

   _____
   _____
   _____
   _____
   _____

6. Is this character friendly or hostile?

   _____

7. Does this character have any special traits or talents? If so, what are they?

   _____
   _____
   _____
   _____
   _____

8. Does this character have certain views about something that is going to happen in the story? If so, what are they?

   _____
   _____
   _____
   _____
   _____

So far you have written a **main topic** on the rough outline, developed a **plot** on the plot development form, and developed two **characters** on the character development forms. Now it is time to develop a **setting** for your story.

Develop the setting

The setting tells **when** and **where** the story takes place. Describing the setting in great detail will make the story more interesting to the reader by making him feel like he was actually there when the story occurred. Use the setting development form on the next page to describe the setting for your story.

Setting Development Form

Where does the story take place? _____

_____

_____

In what time period does your story take place? _____

_____

_____

Does the story take place in the daytime or at night? _____

_____

_____

What does it look like where the story takes place? _____

_____

_____

_____

_____

_____

_____

_____

List anything else the reader needs to know about the setting. _____

_____

_____

_____

_____

_____

_____

Level 7, Lesson 16 – Creative Writing

Lesson 16 Day 2

Date: _____

Creative Writing

You have already developed a plot, a character, and a setting. You will use the information contained in the plot development form, character development form, and setting development form to create the rough outline, the final outline, and the creative story.

Outlining Process

The entire outlining process is explained in **Appendix B**. If you need help in completing the rough outline or the final outline, use Appendix B. Whether or not you use Appendix B first, you still need to complete the rough outline and the final outline on the following pages.

Complete the rough outline
===

Rough Outline

Main Topic:

_____

_____

_____

Subtopic #1: _____

    Details: _____

    _____

    _____

Subtopic #2: _____

    Details: _____

    _____

    _____

Subtopic #3: _____

    Details: _____

    _____

    _____

Subtopic #4: _____

    Details: _____

    _____

    _____

Complete the final outline

Final Outline

Introductory Paragraph:

_____
_____
_____
_____
_____

Subtopic #1:

Topic Sentence:

_____
_____
_____
_____

Detail Sentences:

_____
_____
_____
_____
_____
_____
_____
_____

Ending Sentence: (written after the topic sentence and detail sentences)

_____
_____
_____

<u>**Subtopic #2**</u>:

Topic Sentence:

_____
_____
_____
_____

Detail Sentences:

_____
_____
_____
_____
_____
_____
_____

Ending Sentence: (written after the topic sentence and detail sentences)

_____
_____
_____

Subtopic #3:

Topic Sentence:

_____
_____
_____
_____

Detail Sentences:

_____
_____
_____
_____
_____
_____
_____
_____

Ending Sentence: (written after the topic sentence and detail sentences)

_____
_____
_____
_____

Subtopic #4:

Topic Sentence:

_____
_____
_____
_____

Detail Sentences:

_____
_____
_____
_____
_____
_____
_____

Ending Sentence: (written after the topic sentence and detail sentences)

_____
_____
_____

Concluding Paragraph:

_____
_____
_____
_____
_____

Lesson 16 Day 3

Date: _____

Creative Writing

Drafting Process

Complete the rough draft

So far you have spent quite a bit of time filling out the rough outline and the final outline. As a result, your final outline has all of the necessary pieces to complete your writing.

If you think of something you want to add while you are writing your rough draft, please do so.

Start by writing your **introductory paragraph**, sentences for each **subtopic** (topic sentence, detail sentences, and ending sentence), and **concluding paragraph** on the lines below.

_____
_____
_____
_____
_____
_____
_____
_____
_____
_____
_____
_____
_____
_____
_____

Lesson 16
Day 4

Date: _____

Creative Writing

Edit the rough draft

It is now time to **edit** the rough draft you wrote on Day 3. Use the edit marks shown in **Appendix C** to correct any mistakes.

Do your paragraphs say what you want them to say? Do the words you chose make sense?

Look for and fix the following errors: 1) incorrectly used, misspelled, or misplaced words, 2) incorrect or missing spacing, 3) incorrect, missing, or misplaced punctuation, and 4) incorrect or missing capitalization.

Lesson 16 Day 5

Date: _____

Creative Writing

Complete the final draft

On Day 4 you edited your rough draft. Today you will rewrite your story in its final draft form.

Read your story one more time. Do your sentences flow well from one to the other? Does your entire story make sense? Can you make it even better by adding 1) **time order words**, 2) **strong verbs**, 3) **adverbs**, 4) **exact nouns**, 5) **descriptive adjectives**, 6) **metaphors**, 7) **similes**, 8) **analogies**, 9) **personification**, 10) **hyperbole**, 11) **oxymoron**, 12) **alliteration**, or 13) **onomatopoeia**? Rewrite your edited paragraphs below.

_____
_____
_____
_____
_____
_____
_____
_____
_____
_____
_____
_____
_____
_____
_____
_____
_____
_____
_____
_____

Lesson 17 Day 1

Date: _____

Creative Writing

Develop and write another six paragraph **creative story** using the following three processes:

Story Process
- A. Develop the plot
- B. Develop the characters
- C. Develop the setting

Outlining Process
- A. Complete the rough outline
- B. Complete the final outline

Drafting Process
- A. Complete the rough draft
- B. Edit the rough draft
- C. Complete the final draft

Story Process

Choose one **or more** samples from each of the characters, settings, and plots below. Write a creative story using your selections.

- **Characters**:

  1) a treasure hunter, 2) a detective, 3) a mathematician, 4) a grandfather, or 5) a realtor

- **Settings**:

  1) an office building, 2) a houseboat, 3) a quiet neighborhood, 4) a baseball game, or 5) a farm

- **Plots**:

  1) this character has a hidden power, 2) there were many more of them than he had expected, 3) his decision had worldwide consequences, 4) it looked like the end was near, or 5) she could not believe that happened

After assembling your selections, think of a **main topic** and write it in the main topic section of the rough outline found in the lesson on Day 2.

Level 7, Lesson 17 – Creative Writing

Develop the plot

The plot tells what happens in your story. Without a plot, your characters could exist, but they would have nothing to do. A plot tells what happens next, to whom it happens, why it happens, when it happens, and where it happens. The plot is the foundation upon which the entire story is built.

Usually the plot contains a **turning point** somewhere in the story. The turning point is the part of the plot that is the climax of the story, the part of the story where everything changes, or the part of the story when suddenly everything makes sense. Usually things start out slowly in a story and then build up to the turning point.

Sometimes the **characters** or **setting** are developed before the **plot**. It really depends on the preference of the writer.

Use the **plot development form** on the next page to write ideas for the plot of your story. Do not try to write a story on this form. The plot development form is only used to get you to think about the main flow of your story. "This happens, then that happens, then this happens, *and so on....*" Remember, your plot should be related to the main topic you already wrote on the rough outline.

Plot Development Form

So far you have written a **main topic** on the rough outline and developed a related **plot** on the plot development form. Now it is time to develop characters for your story.

Develop the characters

What types of things do we need to know to develop a character? It depends on the story being told, but knowing the types of things listed on the character development form usually helps develop a character.

For this exercise you will develop two characters of your choice. Use your imagination and create some ideas to describe these characters. Two character development forms have been provided on the next two pages to assist you in developing your characters.

Character Development Form

1. What is the character's name? _____

2. Is this character human? _____

3. Is this character a male or female? _____

4. Where is this character from? _____

5. What does this character look like? (height, weight, hair color, physical characteristics)
   _____
   _____
   _____
   _____
   _____

6. Is this character friendly or hostile? _____

7. Does this character have any special traits or talents? If so, what are they?
   _____
   _____
   _____
   _____
   _____

8. Does this character have certain views about something that is going to happen in the story? If so, what are they?
   _____
   _____
   _____
   _____
   _____
   _____
   _____

Character Development Form

1. What is the character's name? _____

2. Is this character human? _____

3. Is this character a male or female? _____

4. Where is this character from? _____

5. What does this character look like? (height, weight, hair color, physical characteristics)

   _____
   _____
   _____
   _____
   _____

6. Is this character friendly or hostile? _____

7. Does this character have any special traits or talents? If so, what are they?

   _____
   _____
   _____
   _____

8. Does this character have certain views about something that is going to happen in the story? If so, what are they?

   _____
   _____
   _____
   _____
   _____
   _____

Level 7, Lesson 17 – Creative Writing

So far you have written a **main topic** on the rough outline, developed a **plot** on the plot development form, and developed two **characters** on the character development forms. Now it is time to develop a **setting** for your story.

Develop the setting

The setting tells **when** and **where** the story takes place. Describing the setting in great detail will make the story more interesting to the reader by making him feel like he was actually there when the story occurred. Use the setting development form on the next page to describe the setting for your story.

Setting Development Form

Where does the story take place? _____
_____
_____

In what time period does your story take place? _____
_____
_____

Does the story take place in the daytime or at night? _____
_____
_____

What does it look like where the story takes place? _____
_____
_____
_____
_____
_____
_____
_____

List anything else the reader needs to know about the setting. _____
_____
_____
_____
_____
_____
_____

Level 7, Lesson 17 – Creative Writing

(Lesson 17 Day 2)

Date: _____

Creative Writing

You have already developed a plot, a character, and a setting. You will use the information contained in the plot development form, character development form, and setting development form to create the rough outline, the final outline, and the creative story.

Outlining Process

The entire outlining process is explained in **Appendix B**. If you need help in completing the rough outline or the final outline, use Appendix B. Whether or not you use Appendix B first, you still need to complete the rough outline and the final outline on the following pages.

Completing the rough outline

Rough Outline

Main Topic:

_____

_____

_____

Subtopic #1: _____

    Details: _____

    _____

    _____

Subtopic #2: _____

    Details: _____

    _____

    _____

Subtopic #3: _____

    Details: _____

    _____

    _____

Subtopic #4: _____

    Details: _____

    _____

    _____

Level 7, Lesson 17 – Creative Writing

Complete the final outline
=====

Final Outline

Introductory Paragraph:

_____

_____

_____

_____

_____

Subtopic #1:

   Topic Sentence:

   _____

   _____

   _____

   Detail Sentences:

   _____

   _____

   _____

   _____

   _____

   _____

   _____

   _____

Ending Sentence: (written after the topic sentence and detail sentences)

_____
_____
_____

<u>**Subtopic #2**</u>:

Topic Sentence:

_____
_____
_____
_____

Detail Sentences:

_____
_____
_____
_____
_____
_____
_____

Ending Sentence: (written after the topic sentence and detail sentences)

_____
_____
_____
_____

Subtopic #3:

Topic Sentence:

_____
_____
_____
_____

Detail Sentences:

_____
_____
_____
_____
_____
_____
_____

Ending Sentence: (written after the topic sentence and detail sentences)

_____
_____
_____
_____

Subtopic #4:

Topic Sentence:

_____
_____
_____

Detail Sentences:

_____
_____
_____
_____
_____
_____
_____
_____

Ending Sentence: (written after the topic sentence and detail sentences)

_____
_____
_____

Concluding Paragraph:

_____
_____
_____
_____
_____

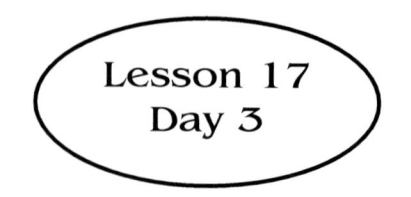

Date: _____

Lesson 17 Day 3

| Creative Writing |

Drafting Process

<u>Complete the rough draft</u>

So far you have spent quite a bit of time filling out the rough outline and the final outline. As a result, your final outline has all of the necessary pieces to complete your writing.

If you think of something you want to add while you are writing your rough draft, please do so. The final outline will now be used as a guide to write a rough draft.

Start by writing your **introductory paragraph**, sentences for each **subtopic** (topic sentence, detail sentences, and ending sentence), and **concluding paragraph** on the lines below.

_____
_____
_____
_____
_____
_____
_____
_____
_____
_____
_____
_____
_____
_____

Level 7, Lesson 17 – Creative Writing

Lesson 17 Day 4

Date: _____

Creative Writing

Edit the rough draft

It is now time to **edit** the rough draft you wrote on Day 3. Use the editing marks shown in **Appendix C** to correct any mistakes.

Do your paragraphs say what you want them to say? Do the words you chose make sense?

Look for and fix the following errors: 1) incorrectly used, misspelled, or misplaced words, 2) incorrect or missing spacing, 3) incorrect, missing, or misplaced punctuation, and 4) incorrect or missing capitalization.

Lesson 17 Day 5

Creative Writing

Date: _____

Complete the final draft

On Day 4 you edited your rough draft. Today you will rewrite your story in its final draft form.

Read your story one more time. Do your sentences flow well from one to the other? Does your entire story make sense? Can you make it even better by adding 1) **time order words**, 2) **strong verbs**, 3) **adverbs**, 4) **exact nouns**, 5) **descriptive adjectives**, 6) **metaphors**, 7) **similes**, 8) **analogies**, 9) **personification**, 10) **hyperbole**, 11) **oxymoron**, 12) **alliteration**, or 13) **onomatopoeia**? Rewrite your edited paragraphs below.

_____
_____
_____
_____
_____
_____
_____
_____
_____
_____
_____
_____
_____
_____
_____
_____
_____
_____
_____

Lesson 18 Review Day 1

Review of Parts of a Story

Date: _____

A. Answer the following questions.

1. What is the **turning point** of a creative story?
   a. The part where everything becomes clear and makes sense.
   b. The part when everything stops.
   c. The part where the characters are introduced.
   d. The parts that describes the setting of the story.

2. Why is a **setting** important?
   a. because it tells how the story ends
   b. because it tells what happens next in the story
   c. because it tells where the story takes place
   d. because it tells who is in the story

3. What is a **concluding paragraph**?
   a. It is the part that that tells how the story ends.
   b. It is the part that tells what comes next.
   c. It is the part that tells how the setting concludes.
   d. It is the part that tells where the story takes place.

4. When should the **plot**, **setting**, and **characters** be developed?
   a. They should be developed after the middle portion of the story is written.
   b. They should be developed before the author starts to write the actual story.
   c. They are not really necessary unless you need guidance.

5. Once the plot, setting, and characters are developed, how are they used by the author?
   a. They are used as the entire story.
   b. They are not used at all by the author.
   c. They are used as a guide to focus the author in writing the story.
   d. They are not to be changed by the author.

Lesson 18 Review Day 2

Date: _____

Review of Dialogue, Point of View, and Voice

A. Below are sentences with **direct quotations**, **divided direct quotations**, and **indirect quotations**. If a sentence is written correctly, simply write the word **correct** on the line. If a sentence is written incorrectly, rewrite that sentence using correct capitalization and punctuation.

1. "Gail said that she needs to go to work."

   _____

2. "What time," asked Jimmy, "will we arrive?"

   _____

3. "Did you asked Tammy, see that bird?"

   _____

4. "Is it time to mow the grass", asked Sally?

   _____

5. David said that he left the costume party earlier.

   _____

6. "Will you iron my shirt?", asked Adam.

   _____

7. "Let's go outside," said Betty, "and play."

   _____

8. Barney said, "I lost a contact."

   _____

9. Ed said "that he wants to take a tour of the factory."

   _____

Level 7, Lesson 18 - Review of Lessons 13-17

Lesson 18 Review Day 3

Review of Creative Writing

Date: _____

Develop a plot, a character, a setting, a rough outline, and a final outline for a **five** paragraph creative story using the following two processes:

Story Process
    A. Develop the plot
    B. Develop the characters
    C. Develop the setting

Outlining Process
    A. Complete the rough outline
    B. Complete the final outline

Drafting Process
    A. Complete the rough draft
    B. Edit the rough draft — Not covered in this exercise
    C. Complete the final draft

Story Process

As with all stories, a creative story needs to have a **main topic** to provide the author with some very general guidance. This time choose one of the following as your main topic:

- a spaceship
- a bucking bull
- a racecar
- a tall ladder

Developing the Plot

The plot tells what happens in your story. Without a plot, your characters could exist, but they would have nothing to do. A plot tells what happens next, to whom it happens, why it happens, when it happens, and where it happens. The plot is the foundation upon which the entire story is built.

Usually the plot contains a **turning point** somewhere in the story. The turning point is the part of the plot that is the climax of the story, the part of the story where everything changes, or the part of the story when suddenly everything makes sense. Usually things start out slowly in a story and then build up to the turning point.

Sometimes the **characters** or **setting** are developed before the **plot**. It really depends on the preference of the writer.

Use the **plot development form** on the next page to write ideas for the plot of your story. Do not try to write a story on this form. The plot development form is only used to get you to think about the main flow of your story. "This happens, then that happens, then this happens, *and so on….*" Remember, your plot should be related to the main topic you already wrote on the rough outline.

Plot Development Form

So far you have written a **main topic** on the rough outline and developed a related **plot** on the plot development form. Now it is time to develop one character for your story.

Developing the Characters

What types of things do we need to know to develop a character? It depends on the story being told, but knowing the types of things listed in the character development form usually helps develop a character.

For this exercise you will develop one character of your choice. Use your imagination and create some ideas to describe this character. A character development form has been provided on the next page to assist you in developing your character.

Character Development Form

1. What is the character's name? _____

2. Is this character human? _____

3. Is this character a male or female? _____

4. Where is this character from? _____

5. What does this character look like? (height, weight, hair color, physical characteristics)

   _____
   _____
   _____
   _____
   _____

6. Is this character friendly or hostile?

   _____

7. Does this character have any special traits or talents? If so, what are they?

   _____
   _____
   _____
   _____
   _____

8. Does this character have certain views about something that is going to happen in the story? If so, what are they?

   _____
   _____
   _____
   _____
   _____

So far you have written a **main topic** on the rough outline, developed a **plot** on the plot development form, and developed a **character** on the character development form. Now it is time to develop a **setting** for your story.

Develop the setting

The setting tells **when** and **where** the story takes place. Describing the setting in great detail will make the story more interesting to the reader by making him feel like he was actually there when the story occurred. Use the setting development form on the next page to describe the setting for your story.

Setting Development Form

Where does the story take place? _____
_____
_____

In what time period does your story take place? _____
_____
_____

Does the story take place in the daytime or at night? _____
_____
_____

What does it look like where the story takes place? _____
_____
_____
_____
_____
_____
_____
_____

List anything else the reader needs to know about the setting. _____
_____
_____
_____
_____
_____
_____

Lesson 18 Review Day 4

Date: _____

Review of Creative Writing

You have already developed a plot, a character, and a setting. You will use the information contained in the plot development form, character development form, and setting development form to create the rough outline, the final outline, and the creative story itself.

A creative story has the following three parts: an **introduction**, a **body**, and a **conclusion**.

- The **introduction** starts the story. It introduces the **characters** and explains the **setting** in which the story occurs.
- The main part of the story is called the **body**. This part of the story may be the most important since it explains what the story is about and tells what happens next. This is also the part that contains the turning point.
- The **conclusion** is the final part of the story that tells how it ends.

Keep these parts in mind as you fill out the rough outline and final outline.

Outlining Process

<u>Develop the Rough Outline and Final Outline</u>

The entire outlining process is explained in **Appendix B**. If you need help in completing the rough outline or the final outline, use Appendix B. Whether or not you use Appendix B first, you still need to complete the rough outline and the final outline on the following pages.

Rough Outline

Main Topic:
_____
_____
_____

Subtopic #1: _____

    Details: _____

    _____

    _____

Subtopic #2: _____

    Details: _____

    _____

    _____

Subtopic #3: _____

    Details: _____

    _____

    _____

Final Outline

Introductory Paragraph:

_____

_____

_____

_____

_____

Subtopic #1:

    Topic Sentence:

    _____

    _____

    _____

    _____

    Detail Sentences:

    _____

    _____

    _____

    _____

    _____

    _____

    _____

    _____

    _____

Ending Sentence: (written after the topic sentence and detail sentences)

_____

_____

_____

<u>**Subtopic #2**</u>:

Topic Sentence:

_____

_____

_____

_____

Detail Sentences:

_____

_____

_____

_____

_____

_____

_____

_____

Ending Sentence: (written after the topic sentence and detail sentences)

_____

_____

_____

Subtopic #3:

    Topic Sentence:

_____

_____

_____

_____

    Detail Sentences:

_____

_____

_____

_____

_____

_____

_____

    Ending Sentence: (written after the topic sentence and detail sentences)

_____

_____

_____

Concluding Paragraph:

_____

_____

_____

_____

_____

Lesson 18 Review Day 5

Date: _____

Review of Creative Writing

Drafting Process

<u>Complete the rough draft</u>

So far you have spent quite a bit of time filling out the rough outline and the final outline. As a result, your final outline has all of the necessary pieces to complete your writing.

If you think of something you want to add while you are writing your rough draft, please do so. The final outline will now be used as a guide to write a rough draft.

Start by writing your **introductory paragraph**, sentences for each **subtopic** (topic sentence, detail sentences, and ending sentence), and **concluding paragraph** on the lines below.

_____
_____
_____
_____
_____
_____
_____
_____
_____
_____
_____
_____
_____
_____
_____
_____
_____
_____
_____
_____

Appendix A
Outlining Process for a Single Paragraph

The **writing process** actually has two parts, the **outlining process** and the **drafting process**. The outlining process is the **act of gathering information** necessary to complete the rough outline and a **final outline**. This appendix will explain only the outlining process. The drafting process will be covered in each individual lesson where it is needed.

As mentioned above, there are two items that need to be completed during the outlining process, the rough outline and the final outline.

<u>Complete the rough outline</u>

The outlining process starts by completing the rough outline. After the rough outline is complete, the information it contains will be used to develop a final outline. The final outline will then be used as a guide to write a rough draft of the paragraph. Below is a sample rough outline that shows its parts.

<u>Rough Outline</u>

- Main Topic
    - Detail #1: (used to make detail sentences
    - Detail #2:   on the final outline)
    - Detail #3:

    [May be more or fewer than three]

Step #1 (develop a main topic for the rough outline)

The first piece of information needed to complete the rough outline is a **main topic**. A main topic is a **very general idea** that tells what a paragraph is about. For example, let's assume we have decided that we want to write a paragraph about **arctic animals**. This bolded phrase is called the **main topic** of the paragraph. Notice that we called this a phrase and not a sentence. A main topic does not have to be a complete sentence. It only needs to be a very general **idea** for your paragraph.

A. When you decide on a main topic, write it in the **main topic** section of your rough outline.

Step #2 (develop details for the rough outline)

Now that we have a main topic (the sample is **arctic animals**), we need to think of **details** to complete the rough outline. A detail is a thought, phrase, or sentence that gives more information about the main topic. These details will be turned into **detail sentences** for the **final outline**.

Assume we possess no knowledge of our example main topic arctic animals, so we conducted some research to gather information from the library, Internet, and some other dependable sources. Our research returned the following **details** about arctic animals:

1. polar bears
2. seals
3. orcas

These are **details** because they provide more description to the main topic of **arctic animals**.

B. Think of a few details for your main topic and write them under the **details** portion of the rough outline. With the addition of your **details**, the rough outline is complete.

Complete the final outline

The next step in organizing our paragraph is completing a final outline that has the following structure:

- Topic sentence:
- Detail Sentence #1: (constructed from the main
- Detail Sentence #2: topic and details in the
- Detail Sentence #3: rough outline)
- Ending sentence:
    (restates the topic sentence and/or summarizes the detail sentences)

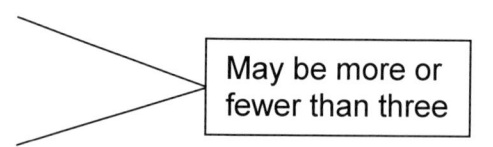

May be more or fewer than three

Step #1 (write a topic sentence)

The first step to completing a final outline is writing a **topic sentence**. A topic sentence tells **generally** what the paragraph is about, but it does not provide specific detail about the paragraph. Its primary purpose is to get the attention of the reader.

By looking at the **main topic** and **details** written on the rough outline, we can use them to think of a **topic sentence** for the final outline. While the main topic in the rough outline may or may not be a complete sentence, the topic sentence in the final outline **must** be a complete sentence. Using our example main topic of **arctic animals**, our topic sentence could be something like the following sentence: **Arctic animals survive very well in the extreme cold**.

Step #2 (writing detail sentences)

The next piece of information needed to build the final outline is detail sentences. Detail sentences will make up the greatest portion of your writing. They actually tell the story of the paragraph. This makes the detail sentences arguably the most important part of the writing.

Look at the **details** written on the rough outline. It is our goal to use these **details** along with the **main topic** and **topic sentence** to think of interesting detail sentences for the paragraph. While you are thinking of these **detail sentences**, remember that they will all need to fit together as a paragraph. By the time you are done you should have several detail sentences written under the **detail sentences** section of the final outline. Make sure to place the detail sentences in the correct order if there is a required order for your writing.

Since you now have all of the information you need to think of detail sentences, write your detail sentences in the detail sentences section of the final outline.

After looking at our details, main topic, and topic sentence from our example (arctic animals), we added some detail sentences to our final outline. Our final outline now looks like this:

<u>Final Outline</u>

Topic Sentence:

   Arctic animals survive very well in the extreme cold.

Detail Sentences:

- Polar bears have a thick, furry coat which acts as a barrier to the cold.
- Seals have a thick layer of blubber and skin that protects them from the cold.
- Orcas can survive in cold water because they have a thick layer of blubber over their body.

Ending Sentence:

   (not developed yet)

Step #3 (writing an ending sentence)

The last step to completing the final outline is to create an **ending sentence**. It is the function of the ending sentence to restate the topic sentence or summarize the detail sentences. For our example above, we could write the following ending sentence:

"As you can see, most arctic animals that survive the cold have blubber or some kind of insulation."

Create an ending sentence for your paragraph and write it on the **ending sentence** section of your final outline. With the addition of the ending sentence, your final outline is complete.

Appendix B
Outlining Process for Multiple Paragraphs

The **writing process** actually has two parts, the **outlining process** and the **drafting process**. The outlining process is the **act of gathering information** necessary to complete the rough outline and a **final outline**. This appendix will explain only the outlining process. The drafting process will be covered in each individual lesson where it is needed.

As mentioned above, there are two items that need to be completed during the outlining process, the rough outline and the final outline.

You will notice that the outlining process for writings with multiple paragraphs is a bit different than the outlining process for a single paragraph. Here are the differences between the two:

1. When multiple paragraphs are required in a writing, they are essentially grouped together to form a larger story or writing. When we have a single paragraph, the reader relies on its topic sentence to tell what the following paragraph is about. In comparison, when multiple paragraphs are grouped together, there is no such sentence or paragraph present that introduces the **entire** writing. Each individual paragraph has its own topic sentence, but none of the topic sentences introduce **all** of the paragraphs. Therefore, when multiple paragraphs are present there needs to be a separate paragraph to introduce or explain **all** of the paragraphs that will be in the writing. This paragraph is called an **introductory paragraph**.
2. The same can be said for a paragraph that concludes the entire writing. Each individual paragraph has an ending sentence, but there is no sentence or paragraph that summarizes the **entire** writing. Therefore, when multiple paragraphs are present there needs to be a separate paragraph to conclude the entire writing. This paragraph is called the **concluding paragraph**.

3. Since many paragraphs are being grouped together, the writer needs a way to identify each paragraph within the writing. The way this is accomplished is by numbering each paragraph as a subtopic. If you look closely at the rough outline or the final outline of a writing with multiple paragraphs, you will see that a subtopic is simply the same thing as a main topic. Of course each subtopic represents a separate paragraph within the writing. As you can see, each numbered subtopic still contains a topic sentence, detail sentences, and an ending sentence.

- - - - -

We will now start the task of completing the outlining process.

Complete the rough outline

The outlining process starts by completing the rough outline. After the rough outline is complete, the information it contains will be used to develop a final outline. The final outline will then be used as a guide to write a rough draft of the multi-paragraph story/writing.

Step #1 (develop a main topic for the rough outline)

The first piece of information needed to complete the rough outline is a **main topic**. A main topic is a **very general idea** that tells what the story is about. For example, let's assume we have decided that we want to write a story about **arctic animals**. This bolded phrase is called the **main topic** of the story. Notice that we called this a phrase and not a sentence? A main topic does not have to be a sentence. A main topic is a very general **idea** for your writing.

A. When you decide on a main topic for your writing, write it in the **main topic** section of your rough outline for the appropriate lesson. On the next page is a sample rough outline for stories/writings with multiple paragraphs.

Rough Outline

- Main Topic
- Subtopic #1:
- Detail #1: (used to make detail
- Detail #2: sentences on the final
- Detail #3: outline)

> May be more or fewer than three

- Subtopic #2:
- Detail #1:
- Detail #2:
- Detail #3:

- Subtopic #3:
- Detail #1:
- Detail #2:
- Detail #3:

Step #2 (developing subtopics for the rough outline)

Your writing will be comprised of one **introductory paragraph**, two or more paragraphs that form the middle part or **body**, and one **concluding paragraph**. This means that you will have to separate your writing into three pieces (introductory paragraph, body, and concluding paragraph).

Since the **body** of your writing will be made up of more than one paragraph, you must develop a **subtopic** (main topic) for each paragraph. Of course this means that each **subtopic** will represent a paragraph in your writing. For our sample story, we have selected three subtopics (your assignment may have more or fewer subtopics) which means that there will be three paragraphs that form the body of our writing.

After adding a **main topic** and **subtopics**, here is how the rough outline for our sample story looks so far:

Main Topic: arctic animals
Subtopic #1: polar bears
    Details: (not yet developed)
Subtopic #2: seals
    Details: (not yet developed)
Subtopic #3: orcas
    Details: (not yet developed)

A. Write the required number of subtopics on the rough outline for your writing. Make sure you write them in the correct order when they occur in your story (if a correct order is necessary).

Step #3 (developing **details** for the rough outline)

Now that you have developed a main topic and your subtopics, you will next need to develop **details** to complete the rough outline. A detail can be a thought, phrase, or sentence that gives more information about the subtopic. These details will later be turned into **detail sentences** for the **final outline**.

Assume that we possess no knowledge of our example main topic arctic animals. With this in mind, we conducted some research to gather information from the library, Internet, and some other dependable sources.

For our sample writing we came up with the following **details** for each subtopic:

Main Topic: arctic animals

Subtopic #1: polar bears
Detail #1: **white fur**
Detail #2: **blubber**
Detail #3: **powerful**

Subtopic #2: seals
Detail #1: **fur**
Detail #2: **thick blubber**
Detail #3: **fast swimmer**

Subtopic #3: orcas
Detail #1: **blubber**
Detail #2: **fast swimmer**
Detail #3: **top of food chain**

Our rough outline is now complete. You can see that by adding details to the rough outline the story is starting to become clearer.

B. Think of a few details for each subtopic in your writing and add them under the appropriate **detail** sections of your rough outline. With the addition of your **details**, your rough outline is complete.

Complete the final outline

You will notice that the rough outline and the final outline **both** have numbered **subtopics** (subtopic #1, subtopic #2, and subtopic #3 in our example) and **details**. The information contained in subtopic #1 in the rough outline (including the details) is used to build subtopic #1 on the final outline, and so on.

We will now start constructing our final outline which has the following structure:

<u>Final Outline</u>

- Introductory Paragraph: (introduces the entire writing)

- Subtopic #1: (can be as many subtopics as necessary)
  - Topic Sentence: (tells about the paragraph)
  - Detail Sentence #1: (constructed from the main
  - Detail Sentence #2: topic and details in the
  - Detail Sentence #3: rough outline)
  - Ending Sentence: (restates the topic sentence or summarizes the detail sentences.)

  > May be more or fewer than three

- Subtopic #2:
  - Topic Sentence:
  - Detail Sentence #1:
  - Detail Sentence #2:
  - Detail Sentence #3:
  - Ending Sentence:

- Subtopic #3:
  - Topic Sentence:
  - Detail Sentence #1:
  - Detail Sentence #2:
  - Detail Sentence #3:
  - Ending Sentence:

- Concluding Paragraph: (summarizes the entire writing)

Step #1 (writing topic sentences)

The first step to complete the final outline is writing **topic sentences** for each subtopic. A topic sentence (the same thing as a main topic for a single paragraph) tells **generally** what the paragraph that follows is about, but it does not provide specific detail about the writing. Its primary purpose is to get the attention of the reader.

By looking at the **subtopics** and **details** written on the **rough outline**, we can use them to think of **topic sentences** for each **subtopic** in the final outline. While the subtopics on the **rough outline** may not be complete sentences, each **topic sentence** on the final outline must be a complete sentence.

A. For each subtopic on your rough outline, write a **topic sentence** in the appropriate **subtopic** section of the **final outline**.

If you would like to see the subtopic sentences we wrote for our sample writing, go to the end of this appendix.

Step #2 (writing detail sentences)

The next piece of information needed to build the final outline is detail sentences. Detail sentences will make up the greatest portion of your writing. They actually tell the story of the writing (each paragraph). This makes the detail sentences the most important part of the writing.

Look at the **details** written on the rough outline. It is our goal to use these **details**, along with the **topic sentences** you just wrote in the subtopics sections of the final outline, to think of interesting detail sentences for each **subtopic** (paragraph) in the final outline. While you are thinking of these **detail sentences**, remember that they will all need to fit together as paragraphs. By the time you are done you should have several detail sentences written under the **detail sentences** sections of the final outline. Make sure to place the detail sentences in the correct order for each paragraph if there is a required order for your writing.

B. Since you now have all of the information you need to develop detail sentences, write your detail sentences in the appropriate **detail sentence** sections of the final outline.

Step #3 (write ending sentences)

The next step to complete the final outline is to create an **ending sentence** for each subtopic. It is the function of each ending sentence to restate the subtopic or summarize the detail sentences of that particular paragraph. If you would like to see the ending sentences for our sample, go to the end of this appendix.

C. Write your ending sentences in the appropriate **Ending sentence** sections of the final outline.

Step #4 (write introductory and concluding paragraphs)

The **introductory paragraph** sets the stage for the rest of the writing. This paragraph may introduce characters or provide other information the reader needs to know to understand the writing as a whole.

> *The paragraph applies **only** to essays:*
>
> By reviewing the information contained in the entire rough outline, it should be fairly easy to draft a well-defined thesis statement. If a narrow **thesis statement** is not obvious from reviewing the rough outline, then perhaps you were too broad with the details that make up your subtopics. If this is the case, go back and further narrow your subtopics in the rough outline by focusing your thoughts more toward the main topic. The thesis statement will become a part of the **introductory paragraph** in the final outline.

Of course the introductory paragraph may also act to summarize the **subtopics** that follow.

D. Write an introductory paragraph in the **introductory paragraph** section of the final outline.

The last paragraph is the **concluding paragraph**. A concluding paragraph is used to summarize the entire writing. It may also be used to tell the ending of what you are writing.

E. Write a **concluding paragraph** in the concluding paragraph section of the final outline.

Your final outline is now complete! Our final outline for **arctic animals** is on the next page.

Here is our completed final outline:

Final Outline - **Arctic Animals**

- Introductory Paragraph:
  There are many animals that are built to not only endure the extreme cold of the arctic, but also to like this type of weather. We will now discuss three of my favorite arctic animals: the polar bear, seal, and orca.
- Subtopic #1:
  - Topic Sentence:
    Polar bears are large animals that survive in the arctic.
  - Detail Sentence #1:
    Although polar bears have thick white fur, their skin is black.
  - Detail Sentence #2:
    Polar bears are able to survive the extreme cold because they have a thick layer of fat.
  - Detail Sentence #3:
    Polar bears are powerful and fierce land predators in the arctic.
  - Ending Sentence:
    Polar bears are able to survive the extreme cold because their bodies are suited to this weather, and they do not have any enemies.
- Subtopic #2:
  - Topic Sentence:
    Seals are mostly water creatures that can survive extremely cold weather.
  - Detail Sentence #1:
    Although seals look like they have slick skin, they actually have thick fur.
  - Detail Sentence #2:
    Seals also have a thick layer of blubber that allows them to withstand the cold.
  - Detail Sentence #3:
    Seals are very fast swimmers, which enables them to escape from enemies.
  - Ending Sentence:
    Seals are very well suited to survive in the extreme cold, although they do have to watch out for predators.
- Subtopic #3:
  - Topic Sentence:
    Orcas are large water creatures that survive in the arctic.
  - Detail Sentence #1:
    Orcas also have a thick layer of blubber which allows them to survive in cold climates.
  - Detail Sentence #2:
    Orcas are very fast swimmers, which allows them to catch prey.
  - Detail Sentence #3:
    Orcas have very sharp teeth and powerful jaws; this places them at the top of the arctic water food chain.
  - Ending Sentence:

- **Orcas are very well suited to survive the cold, and they are the top predator of arctic waters.**
- Concluding Paragraph:
  All animals that live in the arctic have adapted to endure such a cold climate. Almost all have some sort of blubber or fat layer that enables them to withstand the cold. For some, enduring the cold is only part of the battle, especially when they are not the top predator.

Here is how this final outline would look as a written story:

There are many animals that are built to not only endure the extreme cold of the arctic, but also to like this type of weather. We will now discuss three of my favorite arctic animals: the polar bear, seal, and orca.

Polar bears are large animals that survive in the arctic. Although polar bears have thick white fur, their skin is black. Polar bears are able to survive the extreme cold because they have a thick layer of fat. Polar bears are powerful and fierce land predators in the arctic. Polar bears are able to survive the extreme cold because their bodies are suited to this weather, and they do not have any enemies.

Seals are mostly water creatures that can survive extremely cold weather. Although seals look like they have slick skin, they actually have thick fur. Seals also have a thick layer of blubber that allows them to withstand the cold. Seals are also fast swimmers, which enables them to escape from enemies. Seals are very well suited to survive in the extreme cold, although they do have to watch out for predators.

Orcas are large water creatures that survive in the arctic. Orcas also have a thick layer of blubber which allows them to survive in cold climates. Orcas are very fast swimmers, which allows them to catch prey. Orcas have very sharp teeth and powerful jaws; this places them at the top of the arctic water food chain. Orcas are very well suited to survive the cold, and they are the top predator of arctic waters.

All animals that live in the arctic have adapted to endure such a cold climate. Almost all have some sort of blubber or fat layer that enables them to withstand the cold. For some, enduring the cold is only part of the battle, especially when they are not the top predator.

Appendix C

Mark	Use	Example	Final Outcome
✄	Remove/Omit	kitch~~ny~~en	kitchen
⋀⋁	Delete space	the k itchen	the kitchen
⋁	Insert	the k^c hen	the kitchen
⟋⭕	Move as directed	the kitchen (hot)	the hot kitchen
/	Make lower case	K̸itchen	kitchen
≡	Capitalize	kitchen	Kitchen
¶	New Paragraph	The toy was red and the boy was happy. ¶ He played with it.	The toy was red and the boy was happy. He played with it.
⊙	Insert Punctuation	The kitchen⊙	The kitchen.
[ ]	Center	[kitchen]	kitchen
‖←	Move left or right	‖← kitchen	kitchen
∿	Transpose/reverse	kitn͡e͡n	kitchen
#	Insert space	The#kitchen	The kitchen
‖	Align	‖The kitchen is hot. The kitchen is red.	The kitchen is hot. The kitchen is red.

Appendix C – Edit Guide

Appendix C – Edit Guide